KU-000-982

CHILDREN AND DAY CARE

Eilis Hennessy is a lecturer in the Applied Psychology Department at University College Cork, Ireland. She was previously a research officer at the Thomas Coram Research Unit.

Sue Martin is a research officer at the Thomas Coram Research Unit.

Peter Moss is a senior research officer at the Thomas Coram Research Unit. He is also the Co-ordinator of the European Commission Childcare Network.

Edward Melhuish is a senior lecturer in the Psychology Department of the University College of North Wales. He was formerly a senior research officer at the Thomas Coram Research Unit.

All four authors worked on the 'Day Care Project' at the Thomas Coram Research Unit, Institute of Education, University of London. This was a major longitudinal study of day care in Britain involving more than 250 families over a period of six years. The project was financed by the Department of Health.

CHILDREN AND DAY CARE: LESSONS FROM RESEARCH

Eilis Hennessy

Sue Martin Peter Moss

Edward Melhuish

P·C·P

Paul Chapman Publishing Ltd

Copyright © 1992 Eilis Hennessy, Sue Martin, Peter Moss and Edward Melhuish

Illustrations © 1992 Alison Petrie

All rights reserved

Paul Chapman Publishing Ltd
144 Liverpool Road
London N1 1LA

Apart from any fair dealing for the purposes of research or private study, or criticism or review, as permitted under the Copyright, Designs and Patents Act, 1988, this publication may be reproduced, stored or transmitted, in any form or by any means, only with the prior permission in writing of the publishers, or in the case of reprographic reproduction in accordance with the terms of licences issued by the Copyright Licensing Agency. Inquiries concerning reproduction outside those terms should be sent to the publishers at the abovementioned address.

British Library Cataloguing in Publication Data

Day care and development.
I. Hennessy, Eilis
362.712

ISBN 1 85396 184 1

Typeset by Inforum Typesetting, Portsmouth
Printed and bound by Athenaeum Press Ltd, Gateshead, Tyne & Wear.

B C D E F H 9 8 7 6 5

CONTENTS

Contents

ACKNOWLEDGEMENTS

Many people have helped us with the production of this book and we would like to record our thanks here. We are grateful to Marlene Caplan, Harry McGurk, Pat Petrie, Barbara Tizard and Linda Wall for reading the book in draft form and providing helpful comments and suggesting improvements. Mary Ward gave us invaluable technical support with the word processing and printing of the manuscript, and Jenny Martin gave efficient assistance with collating the manuscript. We would also like to thank Alison Petrie for responding so quickly to our request for help and for emphasizing important aspects of the text with her delightful illustrations.

1
INTRODUCTION

Day care is a part of everyday life for many children. Every morning, in Britain and many other countries, young children set off with their parents to go to their childminder or grandmother or to the day nursery, or wait for the arrival of their nanny. As increasing numbers of children spend more time in day care, so increasing numbers of researchers study the development of those children. This is a book about that research. What lessons can we learn from it all? What do we know about the development of children in day care?

Before looking at research, however, it is important to say something about day care itself. There is no standard way in which children are cared for. Arrangements for children's care differ between countries. This book compares day care and day care research only in 'developed' countries; a far greater diversity would be revealed if a description of day care from 'developing' countries was also included. Within countries there are further differences, apparent both at the level of individual families and when comparing families in different social, ethnic or other groups.

Care arrangements also change over time. At the level of individual children, this may mean that they have several different care arrangements in the course of their early years. More broadly, change over time means that patterns of care arrangements change over the years. There may be marked differences in these patterns when comparing different centuries or even different generations. For example, the way in which a child is cared for may differ considerably from the way her grandparents were cared for.

This diversity should be a constant reminder that there is no one 'right' type of care for children, and that the results of any individual piece of research cannot necessarily be applied to all children. Much research is small scale and local and the families or the day care settings studied are unlikely to be representative of the country as a whole or indeed of the city, town or area of countryside where the research takes place. Research mostly takes place over a short period: perhaps a year or two, perhaps in a few cases over five or ten years. In either case the researcher is working at one very specific point of historical time.

In considering a piece of research, therefore, the reader must always ask herself a number of questions. Where did it take place? What type of families were studied? When was it undertaken? The reader must always be aware that every piece of research, and every day care service researched, is situated in a specific context. The findings may well not apply to another context, for example to another country or to another period of time.

This chapter discusses some of the main dimensions of day care diversity introduced above. It also covers the issue of parental choice: why do parents use a particular type of day care for their children? The answer to this question in turn throws light on the reasons for diversity in day care arrangements that exist within countries. Finally, the concluding section discusses the term 'day care', including what is meant in this book by 'day care research', and also the inadequacy of the term when thinking about future directions for the development of services.

Trends in the recent history of the care of children

Victoria was born in 1900 to a family in north London. Her father was a draper and had a small shop which provided a reasonable income for the family. As soon as Victoria was born her parents, like most of their friends, employed a nursemaid. The nursemaid was responsible for taking care of Victoria, including jobs such as bathing her, taking her for walks and ensuring that her clothes were always well cared for. Victoria's mother, who did not work outside the home, was there to supervise and ensure that the baby was well looked after.

Forty years later Peter was born in the same part of London. His father was a junior clerk in the City and his mother never considered doing anything other than staying at home to look after Peter and his two sisters. But Peter had been born during the Second World War and this was to affect the lives of the whole family. Peter's father joined the army and his mother believed it her duty to respond to the government appeals for women to take over the jobs of the men who had gone away. In order to encourage women the government had opened day nurseries all around the country which would look after children during the working day. There was a nursery very close to Peter's home and he went there every day with his sister Elizabeth.

Paul was born in 1950. His father was a skilled craftsman in an engineering works, while his mother had been a secretary before Paul was born. The nurseries opened during the War were now closed and there was little call on women with young children to go out to work. Paul's mother looked after him, and his younger sister, at home until he began school, taking up a part-time typist's job only after Paul had moved on to secondary school. Both of Paul's parents believed that mothers should stay at home to bring up young children.

Emma was born in 1988. Her father was a nurse in a psychiatric hospital and her mother was a social worker. Emma's mother was entitled to maternity leave and took five months after Emma's birth; she then returned to work. Neither of Emma's parents had chosen to stay at home with her after that time. They both had careers which they enjoyed and both incomes were needed to pay the mortgage. Her parents spent a lot of time finding a childminder whom they believed would give Emma the best possible care and they were very happy with their choice. When she was three, Emma's parents found a new childminder nearer home, so Emma could go to the local playgroup two mornings a week where she would meet some of the children with whom she would go to school.

Although none of these children really exists, their stories illustrate some of the care arrangements made for children born in Britain at different periods during the twentieth century. Why does the care of children change in the course of history? The answer is that many factors combine to produce change. The examples given above illustrate a number of these factors.

Economic developments are crucial. Industrialization, for example, led to a separation of the household from the place of work (in the factory or, later, the office). Men went out to work and earned money, women became household managers and financially dependent on their husbands. At the turn of the century in Britain, while women usually went out to work before marriage or if widowed or separated, they did not usually do so when married. In 1911 only about one in ten married women had a recognized occupation, although more may have done work at home which was not recognized in official statistics, for example taking in lodgers or doing laundry (Hobsbawm, 1987).

However, the employment of women with children has continued to change over time in response to economic demands. There were temporary changes during war time, when the call-up of men for the armed forces and the demands of war industries led to a rapid increase in the numbers of working mothers. In the last thirty years or so the number of employed mothers has steadily increased in response to other economic demands.

A second factor which has influenced the care of children during the last 100 years has been the change in the availability of servants. At the beginning of the century most middle-class families in Britain could at least afford to have a nursemaid to help with the care of young babies and children (Gathorne-Hardy, 1972). Those who were better off probably also had a nanny and a governess. But the situation changed, especially after the Second World War. Employment opportunities increased, so fewer women were available to take on domestic jobs. Even if more women had been available the middle and upper classes were less affluent, relatively, than they had been before the War. On the basis of only one earner (the husband), they could no longer afford to employ so many people to look after their children. More recently, and especially in the 1980s, the situation has again been changing. Increasingly mothers have joined fathers in the work-force and this has created a need for someone to look after children while their parents work. Some of these women and their partners are in highly paid jobs and this has resulted in an increase in the number of *dual earner* families in which parents can afford to pay to have their children looked after in their own home.

A third factor influencing the way children are cared for is the availability of services outside the home. The demands of a wartime economy led to a rapid increase in publicly funded day nursery provision in Britain between 1939 and 1945. After the War most nurseries closed. The limited number remaining were no longer for children with working parents, but became a 'welfare' service for children or families considered to have special problems. As employment has increased again among mothers with young children in the late 1980s, there has been no corresponding increase in provision of public services to meet their day care needs. Instead, private day care services have expanded, including a growing number of childminders (Department of Health, 1991a).

The four children described earlier illustrate two other factors which have affected children's day care, though they may be less obvious. First, all of them would have begun compulsory school at age five. Compulsory school has influenced our thinking about children and public services for them. It has also meant that from age five, children spend a substantial amount of time at school where they receive both education and care. Yet this was not always so. Compulsory primary school was only introduced in Britain towards the end of the nineteenth century when the government recognized the need to provide a better educated and therefore a more productive work-force. In order to do this they provided primary schools for children and ensured that everyone got some education by making attendance compulsory.

School attendance may also affect care arrangements through the development of nursery education for children aged around three and over. In this century extensive nursery schooling has been introduced in many countries, but this has not happened in Britain. Nursery education did not therefore figure in the stories of Victoria, Peter, Paul or Emma.

The final factor which has had an influence on the care of children has been the provision of time off work for parents following the birth of a baby. Maternity leave is now a legal right in many countries and reflects a concern with the health of pregnant women and their babies. More recently parental leave has begun to be introduced in a number of developed countries. Parental leave begins after the end of maternity leave and it gives parents the option of one of them staying at home to look after their baby without having to resign their job. Parental leave is not available in Britain, and maternity leave appeared only in the story of Emma, the one child born since the introduction of this type of leave.

The five factors outlined above are by no means an exhaustive account of why changes in care arrangements have occurred over time, nor have the many interconnections between the various factors been explored. The important point to emphasize is that the way in which children are cared for, and the role of day care services within overall care arrangements, are the products of a variety of economic, social, political and other forces. And just as these forces are constantly changing, so do care arrangements and day care services change, to meet new demands and circumstances, to respond to new sources of supply of services or the decline of old sources.

Four national examples

Nationally, changes in day care arrangements happen at different speeds and in different ways. In order to illustrate these differences, the changing care arrangements in four countries are described in more detail in this section. The selection of countries has been made for a number of reasons. The USA was chosen because most of the research which is described in Chapters 4, 5 and 6 has taken place there. In the USA there is a great emphasis on private parental responsibility for the care of babies and preschool children. A leading American researcher has described it as 'a social system that cherishes individualism and family privacy to the neglect of collective responsibility for children'(Phillips, 1990, p. 161).

In Denmark and France there is much greater emphasis on public responsibility for services for children. Descriptions of their systems help to put the USA in perspective and to illustrate the differences in care systems that arise when day care includes a substantial public service as well as private arrangements. Britain has a day care system that is similar to that in the USA yet there is much greater public responsibility for other aspects of children's care and well-being, for example through the provision of health services and child benefit.

Each example describes recent changes and the current situation in schooling, public and private day care, the employment of mothers and leave allowances for parents. (For fuller descriptions of the situation in these countries, see Moss, 1988, 1990; Melhuish and Moss, 1990; Langsted, in press.)

Britain

In Britain children start compulsory school at the age of five. In the years after this first became law large numbers of three- and four-year-olds also went to primary school. However, this practice declined after 1900 and there was never a sufficient growth in the number of nursery schools or classes to offer places to all three- and four-year-olds. A government commitment in 1972 to provide nursery schooling for all children whose parents wanted it has never been implemented. Even the minority of children who do have places usually go part time. The absence of nursery education services for three- and four-year-olds has led to two developments for this age group: many four-year-olds being admitted early to primary school; and the growth of playgroups, which provide for more children than any other preschool service but, on average, offer only around six hours a week per child.

Britain has traditionally had a low level of employment among women with preschool children, with most employed mothers working part time, often for short hours (less than twenty hours a week). Employed mothers have often managed by working evenings, weekends or nights, leaving children in the care of fathers or relatives. (It should be emphasized that 'relatives' does not include children's fathers. There is an assumption – common in society and day care research – that day care is needed because *mothers* are employed. Our assumption is that it is needed because *parents* are employed and our focus therefore is on non-parental care and on care needs arising from parents' employment. Many fathers provide care while mothers are employed, while even more mothers provide care while fathers are out at work.) During the second half of the 1980s the situation began to change. There has been a rapid growth in the overall rate of employment (from 27 per cent in 1984 to 40 per cent in 1989) and also in full-time employment (from 7 per cent to 12 per cent in the same period).

Successive governments have been reluctant to intervene to provide support for employed parents and their children, defining their needs as an essentially private rather than a social responsibility. Public day care is very limited in quantity and confined to children defined as 'in need', a definition which excludes employed parents (except for some lone mothers). Owing to strict qualifying conditions maternity leave is not universally available, and there is no parental leave.

The main form of care for children under the age of three is that given by relatives, followed by childminders and, a long way behind, nurseries and nannies. Although the number of children who are looked after by relatives has increased during the 1980s, the largest increase has been children at childminders. The actual number of registered childminders increased by over half between 1984 and 1989. In the same period there has also been a rapid growth in private nurseries, whose numbers doubled, though from a much lower base than childminders. Overall, there are still more than three times as many places at childminders as at private nurseries. Use of nannies, mothers' helps, au pairs and other carers looking after children at home has also increased substantially in recent years, although again from a very low starting point. In addition, surveys show a substantial number of two-year-olds in playgroups.

USA

Compulsory school begins at the age of six in the USA but around half the children attend some form of early education after their third birthday. Almost all five-year-olds attend half-day sessions in kindergarten classes in primary school, while other children go to public or private nursery schools.

Employment among mothers has increased rapidly in recent years. Labour force participation among women with a child under twelve months almost doubled between 1977 and 1990, by which time 60 per cent of women with a child under six were employed. Moreover, most employed mothers have full-time jobs.

The USA has neither parental leave nor maternity leave. Day care is mainly regarded as a private matter, except where parents are considered inadequate or poor. The provision of publicly funded day care for employed parents is focused on low income families, with the aim of increasing employment and reducing welfare costs. In addition, the Head Start programme, mainly for three- to five-year-olds, has a long-term goal of preventing poverty by attempting to compensate children from low income families for disadvantaged home environments. There is little publicly funded provision for most employed parents, although the costs of private day care are subsidized, to a limited extent, through tax relief.

Between 1965 and 1985, during a period of rapid growth in maternal employment, the proportion of day care for children under three provided by relatives dropped steadily, as did the proportion of care provided in the child's home by non-relatives. The main growth for this age group was in childminding, which by 1985 provided care for as many children as were provided for by relatives. Nurseries showed a similar growth: whereas in 1965 only one in twenty children attended a day nursery, by 1985 the number had grown to nearly one in four. By 1988 childminding was the main type of day care for children under three, followed by care provided by relatives.

France

France has a long tradition of nursery education, for children from about age three up to compulsory school age, which is six. Nursery schools originally began as 'shelters' (*salles d'asile*) to provide for children with employed parents, but the 1881 law on free primary education placed them in the education system and they became nursery schools. Now virtually all children attend, and most go full time (from 8.30 a.m. to 4.30 p.m.). Many nursery schools also provide care for children outside school hours (often referred to as out-of-school care).

France has had relatively high levels of maternal employment for a long time. Currently just over half of women with children under five are employed, nearly all in full-time jobs. Successive governments have provided support for employed parents and their children, viewing this as an important part of family policy. As well as universally available maternity leave, France offers parental leave until a child's third birthday. However, this leave is unpaid, at least for the first two children. Public day care, in nurseries and 'organized childminding schemes' (where childminders are recruited, paid and supported by local authorities) is for children up to age three, after which they go to nursery school. These public schemes provide for about 8 per cent of this age group, mostly the children of employed parents. In addition, nearly half of all two-year-olds go to nursery school.

Among children under three, relatives still play an important part in providing care, but more children are either in some form of group care (two-year-olds mostly in nursery school, but also a substantial number in day nurseries) or with childminders (either private or in an organized scheme).

As well as funding services directly, the government subsidizes day care costs through tax relief for all parents, plus providing cash grants for parents using registered childminders to cover their social security contributions as employers.

Denmark

Denmark has undergone a revolution in services since the 1960s. Until then few women with children were employed. Since the 1960s the numbers have increased very rapidly, so that today nearly all women with children are employed. Although a large proportion (nearly two out of every five employed mothers) have part-time jobs, most of these jobs involve working twenty or more hours a week.

Before the 1960s there were some nurseries (for children under three) and some kindergartens (equivalent to nursery schools), taking children from age three until compulsory school, which begins at age seven. These services were only given public funding if they took a high proportion of children from poor families. But in 1964 a law was passed which extended public funding for services. The idea of special services for children from poor families disappeared and services no longer had to take low income children in order to be funded. Services, and public spending on these services, rose rapidly and by 1989 Denmark had more publicly funded places for children under school age than any other country outside Eastern Europe. There were places for nearly half of all children under three and more than four out of every five children between three and school age. These places were provided in a variety of services. Children under three went to nurseries and organized childminding schemes. Children from three to six went to kindergartens. In addition there were age-integrated centres for all children under seven and nursery classes in primary schools. Denmark offers maternity leave, two weeks' paternity leave and ten weeks' parental leave, all paid at nearly full earnings.

These service developments and the growth of maternal employment have had a major impact on how children are cared for. In 1975, when fewer than 60 per cent of mothers were employed and publicly funded services were less developed, nearly half of children under six were cared for privately, most (over a quarter) by relatives. By 1989, when employment rates were over 80 per cent, most children were in publicly funded services, while relatives cared for fewer than 10 per cent.

The current situation

Significant features in the care of children at the present time in Europe and North America can be summarized as follows.

An increasing number of children need day care

More and more children need day care as an increasing number of mothers join fathers in the labour market. The need for non-parental care has grown not only because increasingly mothers as well as fathers are employed but also because hours for employed fathers show little sign of reducing in response to increased employment among mothers. This increased need for day care is, however, affected in two ways: by part-time employment and various leave arrangements for parents.

Part-time employment is increasing

Part-time employment is common in Britain, and distinctive because of the short hours worked by many mothers with part-time jobs. Part-time employment is less common, but is growing in many other countries. However, part-timers generally work longer hours than in Britain. Part-time employment is significant for several reasons. Firstly, it raises equal opportunity issues because it is mainly worked by women and is often associated with poor pay, conditions and prospects. On the other hand, the growth of part-time employment has contributed to increased employment rates among women with children. Finally, it affects day care arrangements. Especially in Britain, many mothers work short hours at times when their partners (or perhaps a relative or friend) are able to provide care; hence the large number of mothers who work evenings or weekends and the large number of children looked after by their fathers while their mothers are out at work.

Increasingly, leave is provided for employed parents with children

Nearly all developed countries, apart from the USA, now provide statutory maternity leave for women, to protect the health both of mothers and unborn and newly born children. More recently parental leave has become increasingly common. It is already available in nine of the twelve member states of the European Community and in several other European countries. In most countries leave is unpaid or paid at a low level and 'take-up' by fathers is very low (well under 5 per cent).

The situation gradually emerging is for a parent to be able to take leave (maternity and parental) for all or most of a child's first year. Issues still to be resolved include the length of postnatal maternity leave and of parental leave, to what extent parental leave will be paid, how flexible it will be and what share fathers will take.

Increasingly, nursery school or kindergarten is available for children over three years

In most cases this provision is available for a full school day, though, it should be noted, the length of the school day varies between countries. The emerging situation is that children move into the education system at age three. For those with employed parents the main need becomes the provision of care outside school hours to supplement the care provided at school during the school day. This need for out-of-school care continues up to and beyond admission to primary school, which in most countries begins at age six.

The situation for children under three is more diverse

The development of universal services for children over three reflects a growing consensus that children of this age benefit from some form of educational experience in a group setting such as a nursery or kindergarten. Under three, however, services are still often viewed in a more limited and negative light. They are primarily to provide for children or parents with problems or to provide day care while parents are at work.

The assumption is that parents should normally provide care and that services are needed only when that care is unavailable or inadequate. The idea that day care might enrich the lives of under threes, and might also be needed by non-employed parents, is not widely considered or accepted.

The great majority of children under three receiving regular day care do so because their parents are employed. The remainder are mainly there as 'welfare' cases, because either they or their parents are considered to have some problem. Where are these 'non-welfare' children cared for? The answer changes with time and circumstances. If a minority of mothers are employed in a society, relatives usually provide the greatest amount of care, followed some way behind by childminders, then further behind still by nurseries and nannies.

As the number of mothers in employment grows the picture changes. There is not an inexhaustible supply of grandmothers, or other relatives, ready and willing to provide care. Because the supply of relatives cannot keep pace as the demand for day care grows, the proportion of children cared for by relatives eventually begins to fall and non-relatives become more common as carers. The percentage of children with childminders and nannies grows, while nursery provision is also likely to begin to grow rapidly – either as a result of public funding or because entrepreneurs move in to fill a perceived gap in the market.

With few exceptions, day care for children under three is mostly provided privately and without public funding of services. Parents usually rely on relatives or the private market. In a few countries public funding may be used to reduce parents' costs, usually through tax relief but sometimes by subsidizing the fees.

It is important to note the particular situation of the USA

The great majority of research studies on day care for children have been undertaken in the USA. Public intervention, both in leave provision for parents and day care services, is limited, and education provision for children over three is not as developed as in many countries. There is a heavy reliance, especially for children under three, on relatives and the private market (childminders, nurseries, nannies). As a result there are wide variations in quality and large inequalities in access to services. By contrast, a country like Denmark offers extensive, publicly funded services, so that most children have access to services of good quality. Moreover, Denmark has one system for all children, while the USA has a dual system – some publicly funded provision for 'welfare' cases, and private provision for everyone else.

Choosing day care

Within any one country, what decides the care arrangements made for children? Why does one child go to a childminder, another to a grandmother and another to a nursery? In this section we will consider four of the factors which influence parents' choices. These factors are: the needs of the parents and their child; the availability of services; the cost of services; and the type of care that the parents would prefer.

The needs of both children and parents vary. Although it might be possible to organize services in a way that would meet the needs of many parents, in practice this does not happen. Particular types of service tend to focus on particular groups with particular needs. For example, in Britain a parent in full-time employment who is looking for day care for her child may be able to consider a day nursery, a childminder or a nanny. Playgroups and nursery classes, because of their shorter hours, would not provide care for her child for the whole working day.

The choice of day care arrangement is also influenced by what is available in a particular area. Some parents may live close to relatives who are able and willing to provide care, others may not. Publicly funded day nurseries or organized childminding schemes are on offer to many Danish parents, but to very few British parents. As well as differences between countries in the services available there are also differences within countries. For example, in Britain there are large variations between local authorities in the number of places available in nursery education or in day nurseries.

Availability is determined not only by what services exist locally, but by parental resources. Parents' income and circumstances (for example, the number of children) and the cost of services affect the options available to them. A low-paid single parent is unlikely to be able to consider choosing a nanny or private day nursery for her baby at prices of over £100 per week. A working-class family with two children will not have as much money to spend on day care as a family with one child where both parents are in professional or managerial jobs. There are also other types of resources, for example access to information and the means to take advantage of information. Parents whose first language is not English may have difficulty finding out about what day care is available in their area. Parents who do not have a telephone or a car may be limited in choice because they are not able to contact or visit the available places.

If parents have the opportunity to choose between available day care services they will be able to express their preferences. This may mean choosing between two childminders based on which one the parents like best or it may mean rejecting an offer of care from a relative that a parent dislikes or feels is not right for her child. These are choices at an individual level but day care choices also vary between social groups. For example, in Sweden middle-class parents make greater use of public services, especially group care in publicly funded nurseries. Working-class parents are more likely to prefer some form of home-based care, either by a parent, or else a relative or childminder. This seems to have little to do with the availability of services. More important are the different attitudes to day care held by the different social classes (Broberg and Hwang, 1990). Similar social differences in day care choices have been found in other places where publicly funded services are widely available (Moss, 1988; Leprince,1990). In most countries day care provided by relatives is more common among children whose parents have lower incomes and lower status jobs.

In the USA there is evidence of some relationship between ethnicity and the use of different types of day care. In particular, black mothers are more likely than white mothers to rely on care provided by relatives and are less likely to use nannies (Phillips, 1990; Dawson, 1990). However, this may be due to black mothers having fewer resources because it has also been found that lower income mothers are more likely to rely on care provided by relatives. Less evidence exists in European countries about the relationship between ethnicity and day care use. What there is points to more use of relatives by minority ethnic groups. The research also shows that the proportion of children attending day care varies considerably according to ethnic group. In Sweden and France, for example, employment rates among women from Turkey and North Africa are low so very few of these children are in day care (Broberg and Hwang, 1990; Leprince, 1990). In Britain mothers in some minority ethnic groups, for example Afro-Caribbeans, have higher levels of employment than white mothers, while other groups, for example Pakistanis or Bangladeshis, are less likely to be employed (Central Statistical Office, 1991).

For parents who prefer childminders or relatives, it is this one-to-one relationship, and the more individual and 'home-like' care that the relationship is believed to offer, that is the major attraction. In addition, relatives are an attractive option to some parents because of the close existing relationship between relative, parent and child, and the trust that goes with such a relationship. Parents who choose nurseries usually like the fact that their child has the chance to be with other children. Nurseries also provide a particular type of staffing, supervision, facilities and range of activities as well as a guarantee of continuity. Children in nurseries mix with many children and adults and are therefore less likely to form a close relationship with just one other person. Some parents are influenced in their choice because they believe that nursery care is, therefore, not such a threat to the mother–child relationship.

Studies of parental preference consistently show that a substantial proportion of parents are not using the type of care that they say they would prefer. This type of research can be useful when discussing services that could be provided in the future but also needs to be treated with caution. When people are asked what type of service they want their answer will be determined by the services they know about, by what they expect and by the services which the interviewer mentions. Finally, parents' preferences change over time as social and economic conditions change. In the circumstances, the best we can say is that parents with children around the age of three and over generally express a preference for some form of group experience, usually in nursery school or kindergarten. For children under three, many parents prefer more individual care – by a relative or childminder or nanny – but a significant proportion want and value group care.

Day care histories

Change is inevitable in the arrangements that parents make for children's care. Children in all countries enter primary school between the ages of five and seven and many begin attending nursery school or kindergarten around age three. But research is now showing that children often experience many other changes such as moving from one childminder to another or moving from a relative to a childminder. Because these changes are specific to an individual child we refer to them as a child's *day care history*.

How often do children experience change? In the Thomas Coram Research Unit project in Britain (described in Chapter 3) nearly half of all children in day care experienced at least one change before they reached age three. Nearly a quarter had two or more changes (Brannen and Moss, 1990). A recent American project reported that a quarter of children under three had changed day care arrangements at least once in the preceding year (Dawson, 1990).

What factors influence these changes? Children looked after by just one person (a childminder, a relative or a nanny) are most likely to experience changes in day care. This is hardly surprising. Since the care is dependent on one person, any changes in that person's life (for example, illness, moving house, the birth of a baby) will affect the day care arrangement. In the Thomas Coram Research Unit project, placements with a childminder or with a relative were nearly twice as likely as nursery placements to end in a child being moved. A major reason for both relative and childminder placements ending was because the carer's circumstances changed (for example, she moved house or got another job) or because the carer felt unable to cope with the child.

Other factors also contribute to the likelihood of change in arrangements made with childminders (the one group of individual carers who have been studied (Mayall and Petrie, 1977)). Many childminders enter the work on a temporary basis, while they themselves have young children. The fact that pay and conditions are poor, together with increasing employment opportunities elsewhere create conditions where they are likely to look for other jobs. Recent research in the USA suggests that over half of all childminders leave the work every year (Clarke-Stewart, 1991), and there is also evidence of high turnover among childminders in parts of Britain (Moss, 1987).

Although children in day nurseries or other types of group care are less likely to experience an actual change of placement, group care has its own form of instability, due to turnover among nursery workers. A child may stay in one nursery but at the same time experience care by a large number of workers over a two- or three-year period. Unfortunately, there is little hard evidence about this. We do not know how many carers children have during their time in group care. That it can be a substantial problem is revealed by a recent large-scale study of nursery workers in the USA – the National Child Care Staffing Study (Whitebook, Howes and Phillips, 1989) – which reported a high turnover rate among nursery staff. In a one-year period four out of every ten nursery workers left their jobs.

This American project found that turnover rates were related to pay and conditions. The better the pay and conditions, the lower the turnover. Unfortunately, we know little else about turnover – for example, what else may have an impact on nursery workers, or what factors affect turnover among other carers such as relatives, childminders and nannies. We also cannot make valid comparisons for turnover, and stability of care, between countries where nursery workers and childminders have relatively good pay, conditions and training (such as Denmark) and the more common situation where pay, conditions and training are relatively poor.

Researchers have just begun to investigate the way in which changes in day care arrangements (also called day care stability) influence children's development. Change is potentially a positive experience offering new opportunities to the child. But the results of research also suggest that change can be harmful. Chapters 4, 5 and 6 discuss the results of a number of projects which have found that a large number of changes in day care arrangements may have negative effects on aspects of children's development. More research is needed to discover what conditions are likely to foster stable care arrangements.

Finally, to complete this picture of the complexity of day care arrangements, many children have multiple care arrangements. Because of the length of the school day and long school holidays, many children at school require additional out-of-school care – with a relative, childminder or in a centre (for example, an after-school club or a holiday club). But even before children start school, many parents put together arrangements with two or more components. As yet no research has been done on how common these arrangements are or what their likely impact is on the developing child. As with change there is potential for positive and negative consequences arising from these arrangements. On the positive side children may benefit from having many different experiences. On the negative side a child's many carers might be inconsistent in how they treat her or in what they expect of her. Under these circumstances a child may well become confused about how she should behave.

Day care and preschool education

It has been common to divide services for children into two groups: day care and preschool education. Preschool education has usually meant children over three in nursery education or kindergartens. Day care has meant children under three and, more broadly, children receiving full-time care in nurseries, with childminders or relatives – in other words in a 'non-school' setting. This division has affected services and research. Major inconsistencies have developed between day care and preschool education services, in funding, cost to parents, availability, hours of opening, orientation, administrative responsibility, the training and pay of workers and so on. Research on preschool education has tended to look for possible positive consequences of attending nursery school and similar provision for children over three. Research shows that 'preschool programmes can bring about beneficial outcomes, especially in children from disadvantaged backgrounds' (Education Select Committee, 1989a, p. 238). Such findings contributed to a Select Committee of the House of Commons concluding that preschool education 'can not only enrich the child's life at the time but can also prepare the child for the whole process of schooling' (Education Select Committee, 1989b, p. x). However, day care research has been more ambivalent in its focus, paying considerable attention to more negative questions – in particular, is early day care bad for children?

This division between day care and preschool education in services for children, both under and over three, is being increasingly questioned. There is growing awareness that care and education for children are really inseparable and that 'the younger the child the more impossible it is to separate these two components' (Burns, 1989, p. 3). This is leading to reforms in the organization of services. In Denmark, as in Sweden, services for children under seven have two explicit objectives: to provide safe and secure care and to foster children's development. All services are the responsibility of one department (social affairs) and there is an integrated system of staff training. Elsewhere, for example in Spain, New Zealand, parts of Italy and some local authorities in Britain, moves are under way to consider services for all children under compulsory school age within an educational framework.

These developments challenge our thinking about services and in particular the old idea of separate services providing for separate groups of children and separate purposes ('day care' for children with 'working parents', 'preventive' services for children 'in need', 'preschool education' for 'over threes'). They also challenge the very language that is used to describe services – terms such as 'childcare', 'day care' and 'nursery education' reflect and reinforce a narrow and fragmented perspective. Instead, we need new words (for example 'early childhood services') to describe a more holistic approach, in which services are flexible and multifunctional, meeting the diverse needs of children and carers and integrating care, education and play.

The organization of the book

Having discussed the context of research in this chapter, Chapter 2 focuses on day care in Britain and describes in some detail the day care arrangements of seven children. The varied experiences of the children may help the reader to appreciate the complexity of day care arrangements and hence the difficulty in understanding the relationship between day care and development.

Chapter 3 considers the problems of doing research on day care and interpreting the findings of research. The chapter also introduces a number of day care studies whose results are discussed in later chapters.

Chapters 4 to 6 describe the results of studies which have been concerned with the effects of day care on the development of children. In choosing which studies should be included it has been necessary to confront the division between day care and preschool education discussed in the last section. We chose to focus on studies of children in day care: by this we mean mainly studies of children under three, but also, in some cases, studies of children over three in day nurseries or looked after by individual carers (a situation which is most common in countries such as

Britain and the USA which do not have nursery education provision for most children over three). However, the conclusions from day care and preschool education research are beginning to point in the same direction: to emphasize the potential benefits of attendance, particularly for children from disadvantaged backgrounds, but to recognize that these benefits require certain conditions if they are to be achieved.

Summary

(1) Day care for children differs over time and between and within countries so results of research may not be generalizable to all times and all places.
(2) Significant features of the care of children in Europe and North America include the development of maternity and parental leave, more day care for children under age three, and a movement toward nursery education for most children over three.
(3) Care arrangements made by parents for individual children are affected by a number of factors, including need, availability of services, and parental resources and preferences.
(4) The division between 'day care' and 'preschool education' in services for children under and over three is being increasingly questioned.

Suggested further reading

Melhuish, E. C. and Moss, P. (eds.) (1991) *Day Care for Young Children: International Perspectives*. Routledge, London.

2

CHILDREN'S EXPERIENCES IN DAY CARE

The last chapter introduced the idea of context in day care research: day care means different things in different countries and at different periods in time. This chapter focuses on just one context: day care in London in the 1980s. The day care arrangements of seven children of about eighteen months old are described. The descriptions are drawn from the Thomas Coram Research Unit project (described in Chapter 3) and illustrate some of the issues raised in the last chapter: parental choice, continuity in day care arrangements, changing arrangements and multiple care arrangements. Because of the design of the project some types of day care are not included in these descriptions. None of the children attended a local authority day nursery or was looked after by a nanny.

Day nurseries

Private day nurseries vary enormously in their size, organization and the style of care they provide for the children. The two that are described here grouped their children in a similar way but otherwise offered the children and their families very different types of care.

Rachel at Riverside Nursery

Background

Rachel's parents, Anna and John, wanted Rachel to be cared for in a structured environment with trained staff. They believed that a day nursery would best provide this type of care for Rachel and, as they were fortunate enough to have access to a workplace nursery through John's work, they never really considered anything else. Rachel started at the nursery when she was six months old, at the end of her mother's maternity leave, and spent forty-five hours a week there. John was very involved in the running of the nursery through his work on the committee so he spent a considerable amount of time there and knew the staff and children well. This may have contributed to the parents' very positive feelings about the nursery. However, it was clearly a warm and welcoming place as this account from Anna shows.

> We both feel Riverside is wonderful. The feeling of being part of the place and how concerned they are. They really love Rachel, they're so interested. You go to pick Rachel up and they give you a run-down of what's happened . . . and in the mornings although you can't hand over the kids till 8.30 you can more or less turn up any time, make yourself a cup of coffee, play with your own children, meet the other kids, have a chat to the staff. Whereas some [nurseries] I know you stand outside come rain or shine, until the doors open.

Getting there

Rachel's day started in a way that most adults would find quite daunting: she had a forty-five-minute journey on the London Underground in the rush hour in order to get to the nursery. Her father pushed her in a buggy to the station and although they always managed to get seats in the train it was a crowded, unpleasant journey. They arrived at the nursery at about 8.30 a.m. and John then spent a few minutes settling Rachel in and chatting to the staff.

Accommodation

Rachel's nursery was housed in a temporary prefabricated building while a new building was being prepared. In spite of this it provided excellent accommodation and was only lacking an outdoor play area. This was overcome to some extent by regular trips to nearby parks and open spaces, but not having a safe private garden was clearly a disadvantage, particularly in the summer.

The children were in three groups according to age: the youngest group, 'the babies', had a large room and adjoining bathroom (Rachel was part of this group); 'the toddlers', aged from about eighteen to thirty months, formed another group, again with their own bathroom; and the children over thirty months, known as 'the biggies', were the last group. Each group had its own room which was well equipped with a good selection of toys and equipment suitable for the age of the children.

The carers

The nursery employed eight staff full time and one part time, all of whom had childcare qualifications, for example nursery nurse training. Each member of staff was assigned to one group of children. The baby room was normally assigned three staff for the six children there. The Riverside staff genuinely liked the children they worked with and showed a thoughtful interest in them, their growth and development and their families. There was a feeling of mutual trust and support between the staff and parents. The commitment of the staff to their job and the children was reflected in the relatively low turnover. In the year that Rachel had been at the nursery she had come into close contact with only four staff, the fourth only because she was in the process of moving to the toddler room from the baby room.

The routine

For the first hour or so after the children arrived in the baby room they were involved in quiet play with any of the toys they wanted until about 10.00 when they went out for a walk or had more intensive and organized play, for example with paints or water. Before lunch the children had their nappies changed or went to the toilet. One member of staff had the children in a circle doing songs and action rhymes while the other two members of staff took each child individually to the bathroom. The children were encouraged to do as much as possible for themselves, such as getting a clean nappy from the cupboard, and during the whole process there was friendly conversation going on between the adult and the child. Between 11.30 and 12.00 they had lunch in the baby room followed by an hour's sleep.

To allow for different sleeping patterns and waking times an hour of quiet play took place between 1.00 and 2.00. Unless the weather was very bad the next hour and a half would almost always be taken up with a trip to the park or a walk. At 3.30 the whole nursery joined up for a snack in the toddler room. Those that wanted to sleep (this included Rachel) then had another rest while the older children watched television, played or were read stories until they were collected.

Rachel's father came for her at about 5.30 and after a brief chat with the staff he and Rachel set off. By about 6.30 they were usually home and ready to eat the meal Rachel's mother had prepared in the time since she had arrived home. Two hours later Rachel was ready for bed and she was generally asleep by 9.00.

Jamie at the Garden Nursery

Background

Jamie's mother was a staff nurse and Jamie had attended the nursery since he was three months old. She thought that a day nursery would ensure that Jamie was looked after by qualified staff and that his development would be helped by spending time with other children. On a more practical level she was also concerned to find day care that would allow her to continue her shift work. The opening hours of the Garden Nursery were particularly designed to help shift workers which meant Jamie's mother was able to fulfil her work commitments relatively easily. At eighteen months Jamie went to the nursery for four and a half days a week for a total of just over forty-two hours.

Getting there

Jamie was brought to the nursery every day by his mother. They usually went by car, a journey of about fifteen minutes.

Accommodation

The nursery was housed in a large Victorian building in its own grounds. The children were in three groups according to their age; Jamie was in the middle or 'toddler group'. The toddlers' room was a small L-shaped room so one person could never see the whole area. As there was often only one adult in the room (even though there were usually at least ten children), a partition was used to close off the out-of-sight area. This made the room much smaller and very crowded. In the summer good use was made of the gardens which surrounded three sides of the building but when the weather was bad the children were confined to this small room for almost the entire day. Jamie, in particular, found this very hard. He was a self-confident, lively boy who was big for his age and full of energy. He was constantly involved in arguments and was obviously not much liked by the person in charge of the toddler room. Most disturbances were blamed on him and as a result he was often in trouble for things he had not done.

The room was rather drab with one window too high for the children to see out of but little attempt was made to cheer it up with any decorations. There were often no pictures on the walls by either children or adults. Because of the lack of space there were no comfortable chairs for adults. This meant that the nursery workers almost always stood which did not encourage close communication between them and the children. An additional problem in this toddler room was that it had to act as a corridor for people to get from one end of the building to the other. The older children from the next room had to come through the toddlers' room in order to get to their toilets, and any visitors to the nursery had to come through the room to find the supervisor's office. This meant that there were constant distractions and disturbances for the children.

The carers

The nursery employed seven full-time and five part-time staff about half of whom had childcare qualifications. Two of these were permanently assigned to the toddler room and there was often a third, either a part-time assistant or a student. The number of children in the toddler room varied between about nine and fourteen because many children attended part time. In practice, however, there was often only one member of staff in the room. This was partly the result of the poor morale of the staff who made little attempt to conceal their dislike for the job and therefore seized any opportunity they could to leave the room and go on 'errands'. It was also partly the result of the system of toilet training which meant that one member of staff was almost entirely occupied with taking children out of the room to sit on potties. As a result there were many times when one adult was left with as many as fourteen children. Additionally, as there was so little attempt by the staff to engage with the children by talking to them or playing with them this further reduced the possibility for adult–child interaction.

Staff turnover in this nursery was quite high and in the fifteen months that Jamie had been there he had been cared for by six different people. As there was also quite a high rate of sickness among the staff he had contact with considerably more than this because of all the temporary replacements. Although the person in charge tried to get replacements who had experience of working with children she was not always successful, so often the temporary staff had no qualifications or experience of looking after children.

The routine

On most days some sort of formal activity was set up for the children either in the morning or afternoon. This was often run by a student as this nursery relied heavily on students who came for their practical placements. Unfortunately these activities were not always appropriate for the children. On one occasion, for example, the toddlers were asked to sit at a table and thread small beads on to a string. They found this very difficult as they were mostly too young to have the necessary manual skills or the ability to concentrate for any length of time. The adult in charge did not sit down with them but told them to get on with it while she looked in a cupboard for some more string. Because the task was inappropriate the children were frustrated and began throwing beads at one another. By the time the adult had turned round from the cupboard there was chaos. Two children were crying, one very withdrawn child had gone from the table to a corner of the room where she was sucking her thumb and rocking back and forth, and the remaining three had half-heartedly joined in with the bead throwing.

The lunchtime routine of that nursery was particularly difficult for toddlers, especially a lively child like Jamie. At about 11.15 the toys were cleared away and tables and chairs set out. In another part of the room small folding beds with a rug on each were arranged for the children to rest after lunch. The tables and beds took up most of the room so all the children were then taken out to sit on potties arranged in a row in the corridor. They were left there for up to fifteen minutes whether they had 'performed' or not and apart from instructions to 'sit down' or 'stop fidgeting' there was little or no conversation. The children then moved from the corridor to the tables that were set up in their room and were expected to sit quietly 'reading' books for up to another twenty minutes waiting for the food to arrive. Staff did not eat with them but supervised and told the children off when they were too restless.

At the end of the day when most children had been collected the remaining few were gathered together in the baby room. As Jamie's mother worked long hours on four days he usually spent his last hour there. A lot of emphasis was put on making sure that the children were clean and tidy when their parents came to collect them so some time was spent washing hands and faces, combing hair and adjusting clothes. Most of the toys were put away as the staff did not want to be left with a lot of clearing up after the last children had gone home. Jamie was usually collected just before 6.00 and, perhaps not surprisingly, his mother complained that she found him very boisterous and difficult to handle when they got home.

Childminders

The three childminders that are described offer very different types of care. The differences are partly the result of their different styles and their different attitudes to their work, but are also partly a reflection of the different level of services provided by their local authorities and the use the childminders make of them.

Eleanor looked after by Jean

Background

Eleanor's mother, Tina, was a teacher. She found her childminder through a colleague at work whose daughter already went to the childminder. Tina was very committed to her career and was always determined to return to work after the birth. She would have liked Eleanor to go to a day nursery but a brief phone call to her local authority made it clear that no places were available in local authority nurseries for children from two-parent families. She then rang two private day nurseries. The first told her that they did not take children under two years and the second was far too expensive. Tina's husband, Mike, owned and ran a bicycle repair shop and once he was convinced that they had found good day care he was very supportive of his wife's decision to return to work. Tina first visited the childminder, Jean, when she was only a few months pregnant. She liked what she saw and visited again with Mike about six weeks before the baby was due. Eleanor was three months old when she started full time with Jean.

Getting there

Eleanor woke at 7.30, half an hour after her mother who was already up and preparing for the day. As the family lived in a maisonette above the shop, Mike did not have to get up much before he started work at 9.00. Tina took Eleanor to the childminder by car, a journey of about fifteen minutes. From there she had another ten minutes' drive to school.

The carer

Jean, the childminder, was a mother of two school-age children and had begun childminding when they were still babies. As well as Eleanor, Jean was looking after one other child, Ian, who was four and a half. Ian went to playgroup every morning. In addition, Jean's own two children, then aged ten and seven, were around at the beginning and end of Eleanor's day. Jean's working day was from about 8.15 to 5.30 without a break. However, unlike many other childminders, she did get long holidays because she looked after teachers' children. During the holidays the parents paid Jean half the normal fees as a retainer.

Over time Jean became a good friend of Eleanor's family. When Tina became quite seriously ill she helped out by having Eleanor for longer hours or having her to stay overnight if necessary.

The routine

Almost as soon as she arrived Eleanor was put in a buggy to accompany Jean's children to their school. This was only a few minutes' walk but had to be done every day whatever the weather. As she had been going to school with Jean since she was a small baby, Eleanor was very familiar with her surroundings and well known to many of the children and adults there. From school Jean, Eleanor and Ian walked to the playgroup where they always stayed for a few minutes chatting and settling him in. When Eleanor was two years and three months old she started attending the same playgroup and as a result of her great familiarity with the place and the people there she had no difficulty in settling.

Back at Jean's house again, Eleanor played with the toys or 'assisted' Jean with her chores around the house. The morning was the time most frequently used by Jean for trips to the shops or visits to friends and relations. Once a week they went to a toddler group and on other mornings friends and neighbours would sometimes call in. At 12.00 every day it was time to collect Ian from playgroup and Eleanor generally fell asleep in the buggy on the way home. Jean then transferred her to a cot she kept specially for the children she looked after. Eleanor was a good sleeper and slept for at least an hour and a half on most days. This meant that Jean was free to concentrate on Ian and have her own lunch in relative peace. After Eleanor had woken up and had her lunch she and Ian were expected to play quietly while Jean read or knitted for half an hour or so. The range of toys was fairly limited, consisting of a couple of boxes of dolls, cars and a 'Playmobile' set of small figures. The toys were all left over from Jean's children's preschool days. The children were expected to be tidy and clean and put away things when they had finished using them. On fine days they often played in the garden and in the summer a small paddling pool was put out for them.

At 3.30 it was time to walk back to school to collect Jean's children after which there was about an hour of playing before Tina arrived to collect Eleanor and take her home. Eleanor's father often did not finish work until 6.30 or 7.00 and not long after that she was asleep in bed.

Peter looked after by Mandy

Background

Peter had started with a childminder who lived just across the road from him when he was eight months old and Sarah, his mother, returned to her job as a social worker. She had initially heard about childminders from a friend in the mother and baby group she attended and liked the idea of Peter being in a family home. She visited her friend's childminder but after a second visit she decided that there were too many things she was unhappy about so she looked for another one. In spite of her job in a local authority she had no luck with her own Social Services Department. She found them unhelpful and unable to offer any guidance as to what she should look for in a good childminder. She then turned to the local branch of the National Childminding Association which was very active in her area and through them found the childminder who lived nearby.

Sarah had been very concerned because Peter did not like being put down and she thought that a childminder would not be able to carry him about as much as she did. She was also worried because she believed that at eight months babies were more anxious about strangers and less willing to be separated from their parents than at a younger age. In the event, however, Peter settled almost immediately and the childminder was willing to carry him in a sling at least for parts of the day.

Until Peter was about seventeen months old the arrangement went very smoothly. Peter, his parents and the childminder were all happy. Then without any warning the childminder moved away. One Monday morning Sarah found a note on the childminder's door saying that she had moved permanently and would be unable to look after Peter any more. Sarah and her husband between them took the rest of the week off and combined looking after Peter with a desperate search for a new childminder. They were able to find Mandy through the local branch of the National

Childminding Association. For some days Peter showed his distress at the abrupt change, not at the childminder's where he was apparently quite happy, but at home in the evenings when he was inconsolably unhappy for anything up to an hour. However, by a month later he seemed to have settled and the early unhappiness had passed. Peter spent forty hours a week with Mandy.

Getting there

Mandy's house was very close to Peter's so getting there was no problem. He was usually brought by his mother and collected by his father. The distance was so short that they usually walked, pushing Peter in a buggy.

Accommodation

Mandy lived in a Victorian semi-detached house with a small back garden. There was a large lounge with a good selection of toys and equipment. When she first registered as a childminder Mandy received a grant from the borough to purchase toys and she put a lot of thought into choosing a good selection. An easel was permanently set up with paper and paints ready to use. There were plenty of construction toys and equipment for make-believe play and a well-equipped small bookcase with a range of books suitable for young children.

The carer

Mandy viewed childminding as her career. She was a trained nursery nurse and in addition had attended two training courses provided by the borough for people intending to register as childminders. The first of these short courses she had not found particularly helpful as it covered basic information on child development, health and safety and some ideas for entertaining young children, all of which she had previously learnt. However, the second course was concerned with the business side of being a childminder and included information on insurance, charges, holiday and sickness pay and so on. This she found more useful. As a further development of her career Mandy belonged to the National Childminding Association and received their information packs and newsletters and attended their annual conferences. As part of her professional commitment to her job Mandy employed her mother (who lived in the same house) to help her.

When Peter was eighteen months old Mandy and her mother were looking after three other children: a girl also of eighteen months, a baby of nine months and a boy of four years who attended nursery school every morning. In addition, Mandy's own four-year-old daughter was shere in the afternoons after nursery school and two school-age children were collected from school every day and looked after till about 6.00.

The routine

Peter's day with Mandy was partly determined by the excellent facilities the borough provided for its childminders. After being dropped off with Mandy at about 8.30 he was taken first to the nursery school that Mandy's younger child attended and then almost daily to the drop-in centre in another part of the same building. This centre was principally for childminders but was also used widely by mothers and their young children. It was quite usual for Peter to spend all morning there with a good range of indoor and outdoor toys, plenty of space and anything up to twenty other babies and young children and their adult carers. At the end of the morning it was time to collect Mandy's daughter and another child from nursery school and then go home for lunch.

When Peter, Mandy and the other children arrived home at the end of the morning Mandy's mother had a hot meal ready. Everyone sat down together in the small dining room to eat lunch and Mandy's mother cleared up afterwards. Mandy then took the children to the lounge where they played with toys.

Because her mother was able to take care of much of the routine domestic work Mandy could devote her time to providing the children with a stimulating and enjoyable day with a wide variety of activities. However, routine chores still had to be done and Mandy made these as child centred as all the other activities of the day. When nappies needed changing everyone went upstairs to the bathroom and while they were there often spent twenty minutes or more playing with the bath toys. Children who had a sleep in the day used a cot in Mandy's daughter's room and every day there were outings to collect or take children to school. They also made regular trips to the park and shops.

After school when the bigger children were home, including Mandy's fourteen-year-old daughter (and often some of her friends), was a lively time with snacks, some television and free play. Sarah often had to work late so Peter was usually picked up by his father and pushed home in a buggy. This was only a five-minute walk so they were home by 6.00 or very soon after.

Kevin looked after by Mary

Background

Kevin's mother, Jane, was a typist in central London and she found her childminder through her sister. Jane was very close to her sister and was happy to accept her recommendation. Mary, the childminder, began to look after Kevin when he was two months old.

Getting there

Mary's house was on Jane's route to work so she was able to drop Kevin off there soon after 8.00 in the morning. They went by car and the journey took forty minutes. Jane still had a further thirty-minute drive to work.

Accommodation

Mary lived in a small Victorian terraced house in a rather run-down area. Mary was separated from her husband and financial problems made it impossible for her to continue paying a mortgage without taking a lodger. She divided the house so that she lived upstairs and the lodger had the downstairs rooms. However, they still had to share the kitchen and bathroom which was sometimes inconvenient and a source of constant irritation to Mary. The two children that Mary looked after were restricted to the two upstairs rooms. The larger was Mary's bedroom and most of the space was taken up with a large double bed, wardrobe, dressing table and chest of drawers. There was also one armchair, a hard chair and a large television squeezed into the room. There was almost no floor space left. The other smaller room had two cots in it, one chair and a cardboard box containing a small number of dilapidated toys. A stair gate prevented the children from moving along the landing to either the stairs or the bathroom. When Mary wanted to prepare meals or make herself a drink she left the children upstairs where they were completely out of her sight and earshot. During the day the television was always on and the children were frequently told to sit quietly and watch it regardless of which programme was on.

The carer

Mary was a grandmother with four grown-up children of her own. Since her divorce she was in a difficult financial situation and had tried unsuccessfully to get a number of jobs. When it was suggested to her that she could earn some money as a childminder she was delighted and immediately registered with her local authority. Kevin was the second child she had looked after.

The routine

Mary lived in the same borough and less than half a mile from Mandy, the childminder described earlier. She knew about the drop-in centre and had been once but she found taking the children out anywhere difficult as they were 'too naughty'. As a result the two children she looked after spent over forty hours a week in an extremely confined space with almost no stimulation, toys or conversation. Mary appeared too tired and depressed to do anything other than attend to their basic needs. When she spoke to the children it was usually to tell them off (Kevin in particular tried to get rid of some of his energy by jumping on the bed, the girl seemed too passive to do even this) though she did occasionally direct their attention to something she thought was interesting on the television. This had happened too often for the children to show much response and they rarely looked at what she pointed out. Mary did occasionally attempt to read stories but there were few books and because the children had heard them so many times before they could not be persuaded to attend for more than a couple of minutes.

Jane picked Kevin up on her way home from work at about 5.30 and they finally arrived home some time after 6.00. Kevin, who had not had any exercise apart from bouncing on the bed or any outings apart from the car journeys to and from Mary's house, was often not asleep until 11.00. Jane, not surprisingly, described herself as permanently exhausted.

Relatives

More children are looked after by relatives than any other form of day care and yet there has been very little research into this form of care. Relatives may include aunts and uncles, grandparents and older siblings, and the care may be in or out of the child's home. Some relatives are paid for the care they provide but many receive little or no money. The following two examples of day care by relatives are very different though both are out of the child's home.

Michelle looked after by her grandmother

Background

Michelle's mother, Angela, was a bank clerk and had never wanted to return to work. She felt very strongly that a mother's place was at home with her children. Throughout the time she worked she constantly felt guilty about leaving her child and angry about the situation that made this necessary. She went back to work because her husband wanted her to and because it would have been difficult to maintain the standard of living they wanted without her income and the reduced cost mortgage provided by her employer. Against this background it is not surprising that the only form of day care she would consider was her own mother, Michelle's grandmother.

Angela had some concern about the care arrangements. In particular she felt Michelle had too much adult attention and that her parents were not strict enough. Michelle had developed a pattern of having tantrums if she was thwarted in any way and Angela felt that these were always given into. However, Angela and her family were all very close and although she complained about this aspect of Michelle's care she would not have considered any other alternatives. Indeed, by the time Michelle was three Angela had this to say about the sort of care she was getting.

> I'm one hundred per cent confident that she's getting the best possible love and care that she could be getting. It's a lot off my mind. And the fact they've a genuine interest in her development. They'll teach her, take time to teach her things whereas maybe someone else wouldn't take that time.

Getting there

Michelle's day started at 7.30 when her mother got her up and dressed and ready to leave the house. The car journey to her grandparents was only about ten minutes so she was dropped off there by her parents on their way to work.

Accommodation

Her grandparents' home was a fairly new house on a small private estate. It was very clean and tidy with many ornaments and pictures. Michelle had a box of toys that were kept in a cupboard specially for her.

The carer

Angela's mother shared her daughter's beliefs about bringing up children and she gave up her job of seventeen years in order to take on the full-time care of Michelle. Angela's father had fairly recently retired so he was also at home. Angela's older sister and brother were both unmarried and lived with their parents. Although they both worked full time they were inevitably much involved in the care of Michelle.

The routine

Michelle spent all of her day in the company of adults. She had her own toys to play with and was also taken fairly regularly to the homes of relatives who lived in the area. She had her own cot at her grandparents' house and at eighteen months often slept for up to two hours during the day. This was probably the result of Angela's policy of keeping her up late at night in order to spend more time with her. She was often not asleep until 10.00 at night. During the day Michelle usually had at least one and often two or three short outings. Her grandfather often took her with him to the local shops, sometimes they went for a walk in the park and on other occasions they walked along the road to meet either her aunt or uncle on their way home from work. Angela and her husband arrived to collect Michelle at about 6.00 and after a few minutes' chat would go home to get their own meal and spend time with Michelle before putting her to bed.

Michelle's time with her grandparents was by no means limited to weekdays. It was usual for her to spend some time on both Saturday and Sunday in the company of her mother at her grandparents' house. Before Angela went back to work she saw her parents daily so settling Michelle in was never a problem. In fact Angela was upset when sometimes Michelle appeared to prefer her grandmother.

Lucy looked after by her aunt Marion

Background

Lucy's mother, Julie, was a switchboard operator and also did not want to return to work. She did so only for financial reasons. However, she was much more resigned to the situation and felt that her daughter was benefiting from being looked after by others. Julie and her husband were part of a large close-knit extended family. They did not consider any type of care apart from relatives and had no problem making arrangements. Julie went back to work when Lucy was seven months old and at first left Lucy with an aunt who lived just across the road. This worked well for five months. Then the aunt decided to go back to work herself. Julie and David had three weeks to sort out a new arrangement and were delighted when Marion, another aunt, offered to take over the care. The disadvantage was that Marion lived further away and was unable to have Lucy before her two older children had gone to school in the morning. However, Julie's mother offered to mind Lucy for an hour or so in the morning and then drive her to Marion's house.

Getting there

Because Lucy's day care involved two arrangements she had two journeys. She was taken across the road to her grandmother's house at 7.30 in the morning. She then spent the next hour and a half there before her grandmother drove her to Marion's house.

Accommodation

Marion's house was a three-bedroomed terraced house, built at the turn of the century. There was a small backyard mostly taken up with old bits of machinery waiting to be repaired and where Marion's two large dogs spent much of their day. Inside, the house was untidy with clothes, newspapers, and dirty crockery occupying most surfaces.

The carer

Marion had three sons aged eight, six and four. The elder two were at school during the day and Stuart, the youngest, went to nursery school for about two hours every afternoon. Ever since Lucy had been born she had visited Marion's house regularly and Marion believed in treating her just as she would treat her own children.

The routine

Most of the time Lucy was left to her own devices though she was always treated with great warmth and affection. There were plenty of toys around belonging to Lucy's cousins and she had the free run of the house. There were no activities designed particularly for her but as there was nearly always another child to play with she seemed happily occupied most of the time. She slept for about an hour in the afternoons when Stuart, her cousin, was at nursery school.

Marion had many local friends and relations, many with young children, so there were often several other adults and children in the house. In addition Lucy went out twice a day, first to take Stuart to nursery school and then to collect him and the two older boys from school. Lucy was a very lively, sociable girl who seemed to thrive on the company and had not shown any distress at the change in care she had experienced when her aunt went back to work. From frequent social visits Lucy knew Marion's house and family well which also helped her settle straight away.

At about 4.30 Lucy was picked up by either her parents or her grandmother. She was always at home with her parents by 5.00 at the latest.

Learning from children's experiences

This chapter has provided some real examples of the lives of seven toddlers in full-time day care in London. In the short accounts of these children's experiences many of the issues raised in Chapter 1 are illustrated, including changing arrangements, multiple arrangements and the factors which influence parents' choice of day care. Although the main impression for most readers will be the many different experiences of the children, there are also consistencies in the care provided in some types of care settings. Some of these points are highlighted below.

Making arrangements

Some of the parents had an easy time making arrangements for the care of their child, others had real difficulty. Lucy's parents found arranging child care easy because of their large supportive family and the many relatives willing to take on responsibility for care. Rachel's parents also had no problems because they wanted Rachel to attend a day nursery and were fortunate enough to have access to one. Other parents did not necessarily get their preferred type of day care or did not know what to look for when making arrangements.

Changing day care arrangements

Arrangements which were made did not necessarily last long. Peter's change from his first childminder was unusually sudden but evidence from the experiences of other parents in the project is that many arrangements do not last. What may not be so obvious from the accounts is the stress and disruption that this causes to families. Peter's parents were forced to use up a week of their holiday time to find a replacement. The possible reasons for these frequent changes have already been discussed in the first chapter. Some children in day nurseries also experience frequent changes in caregivers because of staff illness or replacement. Jamie had many full-time carers and many substitute carers in his time at Garden Nursery.

The complexity of multiple-care arrangements

Only one of the children, Lucy, had a multiple-care arrangement. The fact that all the people involved in her care were part of a large extended family may have eased the potential stress of such a situation. As children get older multiple arrangements become more common. For example, Eleanor began attending playgroup when she was just over two (as do many other children) thus introducing another element to her care arrangements.

Variability of experience

Perhaps the most striking feature of the seven descriptions is the fact that no two children had the same experiences in day care even if they attended the same type of provision. Peter and Kevin had very different experiences in the homes of their respective childminders. Rachel and Jamie had very different experiences in day nurseries. These differences have implications for the way in which the results of day care research are interpreted. In particular they suggest that grouping together children attending the same type of care may not be valid because they may have very different experiences.

Similarities of experience

Although there are many differences in children's experiences in day care there are also some broad similarities. Children in day nurseries come into contact with more children than most children cared for in the homes of relatives or childminders. Day nurseries are also distinctive in that they are child-centred environments not family homes. In family homes the care of a child must fit into the timetable and arrangements of the family in a way that is not necessary in nurseries. Of course this does not mean that the child in a nursery will not have to learn to conform to some timetables.

Typically, there are also differences between the adult carers in different day care settings. For example, adults who work in day nurseries are more likely to have formal child care training than childminders or relatives but are less likely to be parents. Adults working in day nurseries are also generally younger than other carers. Relatives who act as carers may have a particularly intimate relationship with the children they are caring for and may share many of the parents' values and beliefs.

Two worlds, one child

When children enter the day nursery or the home of their childminder they are entering another world, one which they do not share with their parents (see Dencik, 1989). The world of day care and the world of home may make different demands on children, for example an only child can expect more individual attention from two devoted parents at home than from two equally devoted caregivers in her day nursery. In the day nursery she must learn to share attention. Children's experiences in one world affect how they behave in their second world. So, for example, children who are used to undivided attention at home may find the environment of the day nursery more difficult to cope with than those who already share their parents' attention with brothers and sisters. These facts suggest that to understand children's experiences we need to study children both at home and in day care and to look at how the two worlds interact.

Summary

(1) Parents have very different experiences in their efforts to organize day care.
(2) Change and complexity are common features of the day care experiences of many children.
(3) Classifying day care arrangements by type may conceal many of the differences which exist between individual care environments.

(4) General differences between home-based care and care in a day nursery include differences in accommodation, carers, and the relationships between parents and caregiver(s).

(5) A full understanding of a child's experiences in day care can only be achieved if the child is studied both at home and in day care.

3
DOING RESEARCH ON DAY CARE

In Chapter 1 the importance of the context of day care was discussed. Chapter 2 then concentrated on individual care arrangements within one context. This chapter provides some information on why it is necessary to do research, who does research and how they go about collecting data. The second part of the chapter provides a brief overview of previous issues in day care research and describes some individual projects that will be referred to frequently in later chapters.

Part one: Doing research

Why do research?

There are very many people with lots of experience of working with young children. Why, therefore, is it necessary to do research at all? Would it not be simpler to ask these people for the benefit of their experience and avoid doing research altogether? In this section it will be argued that research can contribute to our understanding of child development in ways that complement the experience of people working with children by providing an account of child development that is broader than individual experience, by testing theories of child development and by contributing to decision-making.

An individual who has worked with children for many years has built up a good deal of factual information about the way that children of different ages behave. The breadth of experience that it is possible to acquire, even over an entire lifetime, is, however, quite limited. Imagine asking two people, with equal experience of working with children, at what age a child first learns to read. One person has worked with disadvantaged inner city children many of whom speak one language at home and another at school. The other has worked in an advantaged area where all the children have access to books at home and parents who have time to read to them regularly. These two people would probably give very different, but equally accurate, answers to the question based on their experience. The advantage of designing a research project to investigate this question is that the project can include children from advantaged and disadvantaged homes, children who have preschool educational experience and children who have not, and so on. This enables the research workers to answer the question based on the abilities of children from a range of backgrounds.

Collecting factual information is not the only aim of research. It is useful to know the ages at which children are likely to smile, to say their first words, to be able to do addition sums or to develop close friendships. It is also important to understand how children learn to do these things and the extent to which their behaviour can be influenced by other people. Explanations for the 'how' and 'why' of children's behaviour exist in the form of theories of child development. Theories offer possible explanations for children's development which are then tested by research so that they can be given support, disproved or modified as necessary. Only by doing this research will our understanding of child development progress beyond a description of the abilities of children of different ages.

Working with children in any setting involves daily decision-making about the needs of children and how they can be met. Although it is always possible to base some decision-making on previous experience of similar situations this is not possible when new situations arise. For example, a childminder with no experience of looking after young babies, apart from her own, may be interested in knowing the best way to help a baby to develop communication skills. Alternatively, for example, a day nursery which has always organized its groups of children according to age may be considering changing to mixed age groups. The nursery staff will want to know what the likely effects will be on the children and the staff's interaction with them.

Questions about child management, child development, day care organization, and related topics are regularly confronted by day care workers and are also questions which researchers may be able to help them answer. The job of researchers is to provide information which will help in the decision-making process. For example, they may be able to say what the consequences of two ways of organizing groups of children in a day nursery are likely to be from the point of view of the children and the staff.

Although research can provide useful information to people working with children there are certain questions that it cannot be used to answer. Take the example of reorganizing a day nursery mentioned above. Research may be able to say what the consequences of reorganization are likely to be but the decision on which system would be the best has to be based on the judgement of the day care workers. Questions like this are beyond the scope of research and must be made by the individuals concerned.

Who does research?

The research on day care which is described in Chapters 4, 5 and 6 was primarily carried out in universities and research centres. As such it is representative of most research on day care carried out in Britain and the USA. This has had certain consequences for research work. Firstly, it was common, until relatively recently, for much research to take place in university nurseries of very high quality. Such nurseries are frequently very different from the other nurseries or day care arrangements in the same area. This meant that many types of day nursery and other day care arrangements were not studied.

A second important point to make about the researchers is that they were mainly middle class and white. This has sometimes meant that they approached their research from a different perspective from that of many of the users of day care or of workers in day care. It might mean, for example, that they placed more emphasis on some aspects of the care provided than the parents of the children might have done. It also might mean that they did not understand the reasons that the staff behaved in certain ways.

Asking questions

Research begins with a question. There are many questions which people might want to ask about day care. To take some examples: How can we encourage children's language development? What situations lead children to behave aggressively? Do parents have access to the type of care they would like for their child? What effect does staff training have on children in day care? These questions are all about day care yet are all very different and therefore the research needed to try to answer them would be very different. If day care workers are to evaluate the results of research then it is important for them to have some idea of the different methods of doing research and of the advantages and disadvantages of each.

Designing research projects

Once the research question has been asked then it is the job of researchers to design a project which will provide an answer. The design of the project will depend on the resources available, on the time available and, most important, on the nature of the question to be answered.

Take the question 'Are four-year-olds who began attending day nurseries when they were babies more sociable than four-year-olds who attended other types of day care?' In order to answer this question it is necessary to compare children who attended day nurseries since they were babies with children who attended other types of day care. There are two ways in which this could be done. The first way would be to find groups of four-year-olds and to find out about the type of day care they experienced when they were babies. This means asking questions about the past and is called *retrospective research.* When enough children have been found who attended day nurseries and other types of day care, it is then possible to compare the children to see if they differ in how sociable they are. The advantage of designing the project in this way is that you can answer a question quite quickly; however, it also has some disadvantages. The first disadvantage is that you have to rely on people's memory of the past. Although parents will probably remember whether their child went to a childminder or a day nursery, they may find it more difficult to remember more detailed information such as how many other children were there or whether the staff were qualified nursery nurses. Relying on memory, particularly memory of some years ago, may mean that the information collected is not as accurate or as detailed as you would like it to be.

Another problem with retrospective research is that you do not know (and you cannot find out) whether the groups you are interested in were different in the past. If researchers find that four-year-olds who attended day nurseries are more sociable than four-year-olds who attended other types of day care they cannot tell whether this is because of differences in day care experience or home experience. More sociable adults may choose to send their children to day nurseries because they think that being sociable is an important skill. It would be reasonable to expect that these adults would, at the same time, encourage their children to be sociable at home. The children who attended day nurseries, therefore, may be more sociable because they have learnt to be so from their parents rather than because of the nursery experience. The only way to overcome this problem is to follow the development of a group of children over time, beginning before they start attending day care. This is called *longitudinal research.*

To answer the question about the sociability of four-year-olds who attended different types of day care as babies using longitudinal research would mean that you start off by finding a group of parents and babies who have not yet started attending day care and follow the development of the babies until they are four years old. Because information has been collected from this early stage it will be possible to say whether or not the groups started out with similar characteristics. The disadvantages of collecting information in this way include the length of time that you have to wait before your question is answered and the resulting high cost. In the example just described you would have to wait for four years, but if, for example, you were interested in the effects of nursery education on A-level results you might have to wait nearly twenty years to get an answer. Another disadvantage is that after waiting such a long time the world may have changed so much that the question or results are not relevant to the children of the day.

Sometimes longitudinal research is designed to evaluate the effects of changes which have been introduced to an environment. For example, in the USA in the 1960s there was a lot of interest in providing stimulating environments for children from very poor or deprived backgrounds. It had long been known that children from such backgrounds were at risk of failing at school. It was hoped that providing early stimulation would decrease the risk of failure. The stimulation usually took the form of a preschool education centre (like a day nursery or nursery school) which the children attended. The purpose of the research was to determine whether children who received early stimulation went on to do better in school and to score higher on developmental tests than children who did not have the benefit of this stimulation. Studies of this kind are called *intervention studies* because they aim to evaluate the effect of some change in the environment.

Collecting data

There are lots of ways in which data can be collected and the best way will depend on what information is needed and how much time and energy can be spent on the process of collection. All methods of data collection have advantages and disadvantages. Some of the most commonly used methods of data collection in day care studies are listed below.

Observation

This involves watching and making detailed notes on behaviour. Observation methods have the advantage of providing very detailed information on how children and adults behave and the disadvantage of being a time-consuming (and therefore expensive) way of collecting data.

Questionnaire

Questionnaires, which are usually written, are useful for collecting information from large numbers of people and they can often be posted making it unnecessary to meet individuals. Obviously, written questionnaires can only be used with people who are literate and they are not useful for collecting more complex information.

Interview

This involves a meeting (or sometimes a telephone conversation) between a researcher and a person taking part in a research project in order to collect information. The interview can be used to collect more detailed and complex information than the questionnaire because the interviewer can ask questions flexibly, can obtain more details when an answer is unclear and can go into issues in greater depth. Because of the time needed to collect interview information the process can be expensive.

Interpreting results

When the data have been collected the next stage in doing research is to analyse statistically and interpret the results. In the way that opinion polls are used to estimate who will win a general election or who would be the most popular leader of the country, researchers in day care hope to understand the development of many children in day care by only studying a few (usually called a *sample*). This is where the importance of statistics lies. Using statistical tests the researchers calculate the probability that their results were chance findings. Usually, if the probability of it being a chance finding is less than five in a hundred, the result is accepted. This probability is often referred to as the *level of significance* and researchers talk of *significant* findings as those which have this low probability of arising by chance.

If the research was designed to test a psychological theory then the researchers will decide whether the results support the theory or not. Alternatively, if the research was designed to look at some aspect of day care services the researchers will decide what the implications of their findings are for the service. The researchers themselves are not the only people to interpret the findings. Once the results are published they are available to a wider audience and readers will have their own opportunity to interpret them. For example, if the research was done in another country the reader must decide whether the results are also relevant in her country.

If a result is significant it still does not mean that it can be applied to all children. In Britain (as in other countries) there are children who live with two parents, children who live with one parent, children who come from different ethnic backgrounds, children who have disabilities (whether physical or intellectual), children who have very privileged life-styles, children who are very shy, children who are very outgoing and so on. If a research project only includes children who come from very privileged backgrounds then the findings may not be relevant to children who come from very deprived backgrounds. If a research project only includes white families with children then the results may not be relevant to minority ethnic families with children. Because it is unlikely that any one research project will include children representing all ethnic groups and from all possible backgrounds almost all research is limited in its relevance to some groups of children. Most researchers recognize the limitations of their results but a person reading research should always ask the questions: Who took part in this research? How representative of the children that I work with is the sample used in the research project? Is the nursery I work in anything like the nursery described in this research?

Part two: Research projects

An overview of day care research

In recent years more and more researchers have become interested in day care and by now a large number of books have been published as well as hundreds of articles in academic journals. With so much written material it might be supposed that every aspect of day care would have been investigated by someone. In fact, instead of investigating a breadth of issues the majority of research projects have been set up to answer the same few questions.

The question 'Does day care harm young children?' has dominated day care research in Britain and the USA until relatively recently. The question changed slightly over time so that more recently the focus has been on children under one year old in full-time day care but in each case the research concentrated on potentially harmful effects. Frequently such research ignored both differences in the day care environments where children spent their days and differences in the families which had chosen the care. With the focus on possible harmful effects these research projects also failed to recognize the possible range of effects of day care. Why should day care be all good or all bad? Would it not be reasonable to expect that children in day care would have some advantages and some disadvantages compared to those at home?

There has only been one situation in which day care for young children was seen as potentially beneficial rather than potentially harmful. This was in the case of children from very poor or deprived homes. In these circumstances researchers were concerned with the question 'Can day care compensate for deficiencies in the home environment?' This initially became a topic of interest in the 1960s. At this time a number of projects were set up to provide high quality, educationally oriented day care for children from very poor or deprived backgrounds. These researchers did not have to confront the problem of a range of day care environments or a range of family backgrounds because the children generally came from poor backgrounds in deprived urban areas and attended high quality day care. The resulting research findings were interesting but relevant to the day care experiences of only a minority of children.

Recently the emphasis of research has been changing and the early question of whether day care harmed children has been recognized as oversimplified (Clarke-Stewart, 1987a). Research in the last few years has been designed to investigate the different ways in which day care and home environments can influence development. This type of research recognizes the fact that day care environments are not all the same, just as home environments are not all the same. Each day care environment needs to be studied in some detail so that its effects on the child can be better understood. One way of doing this has been to measure the overall quality of the day care environment. A number of 'quality measures' have now been published which allow researchers to distinguish between high and low quality care. The measures usually give day care settings scores on such things as health and safety, stimulation, educational activities and adult–child ratio. All the scores are then combined to give a total score. The higher the score the better the quality. These measures are useful because they demonstrate the great variation in day care services.

Equivalent measures of home environment have existed for some time and have demonstrated the substantial differences that exist in the stimulation and care of young children at home. However, such measures are always based on a particular definition of quality. As many such definitions are possible these measures always emphasize one particular perspective. For example, one measure might emphasize the day nursery as an educational environment and give high scores to nurseries which encourage educational activities. Another might emphasize the day nursery as a social environment and give high scores to nurseries in which children are given the opportunity to play with other children and adults. As no objective definition of quality exists, both may be equally valid measures but any one day nursery might find that it has a higher score on one than on the other.

Measures of quality are frequently supplemented with detailed observations of aspects of the day care and home environments. These could be, for example, relating adults' behaviour to children's language development or studying how the conversation directed towards a child at home affects the child's conversation in day care. This more focused approach has the advantage of providing day care workers with more detailed guidance on how their behaviour can affect child development. If child development is to be understood then it is important to include in the studies children from a range of home backgrounds attending a range of day care settings (high and low quality, centre- and home-based, public and private).

Deborah Phillips, an American researcher, has outlined the type of research which she believes needs to be carried out in the future if our understanding of day care is to make substantial progress (Phillips, 1987).

She identifies aspects of day care which have so far been neglected by researchers such as day care as a work environment for adults and day care in rural areas. She also points out that we know nothing about the relationships between caregivers and parents and how these might influence the child in day care. If results of projects are to be widely applicable then, she argues, the projects themselves will have to be based in more than one area so that the range of available day care can be properly sampled. This view of future research represents part of a growing consensus that if day care is to be fully understood then researchers will have to look outside the day nursery or the childminder's home to wider issues such as the interaction of home and day care.

Some examples of day care projects

The research projects which are described in this section are representative of both the early work on day care and the more recent research with its recognition of the complexity of the issues involved. The descriptions are presented firstly to give examples of day care projects asking a range of questions and using different methods of data collection. The second aim is to provide a description of projects whose results will be referred to regularly in Chapters 4, 5 and 6.

The Abecedarian project

This intervention project (Haskins, 1985; Burchinal, Lee and Ramey, 1989) began in North Carolina in the USA in 1971. It was one of a number of studies started during the 1960s and early 1970s which was intended to help families with very low incomes. The aim was to provide high quality day care to children from a very early age in the expectation that this would improve the children's chances of educational success in school.

The project was longitudinal and followed the development of groups of children from a few months old until they started attending full-time school at about age six. All of the 151 children who took part were from deprived backgrounds, most were black, most had young single mothers. What was very unusual about the project was that the children who took part in the project were *randomly assigned* either to a special day care group or to a comparison group which did not receive this special day care. Being randomly assigned meant that the mothers of the children did not choose whether their children went to special day care; it was decided by chance. In most other day care studies parents chose the day care for their child.

The curriculum at the special day nursery emphasized both intellectual and emotional development. The curriculum for intellectual development emphasized language activities, knowing about objects and being able to classify them. Creativity and imagination were encouraged as were skills at manipulating objects and eye–hand co-ordination. The curriculum for social and emotional development emphasized people's needs and feelings, independence, sharing and co-operation. Children who were not assigned to the special day care group either attended ordinary community-based day care or stayed at home.

Many methods were used to study the development of the children. The children's developmental progress was measured about once a year. Children were also observed in the playground, and when they went to school their class teacher completed questionnaires about their behaviour.

Randomly assigning children to the special day care group ensured that all children were equally likely to have the opportunity to attend regardless of their parents' background or home environment. This in turn meant that any differences between the children who attended special day care and those who did not could not be due to differences between their families. But it also meant that day care placement was unlike the real choices which parents with young children must make when they do not have access to many day care settings because of poverty. It is very unlikely that any group which was not living in poverty would consent to having their child's day care arranged in this random way. The implications of the results are limited, therefore, by the unusual nature of the families and the unusual nature of the day care itself. The children were all from very deprived backgrounds, the day care was of very high quality and placement was not based on parental choice so that the situation is untypical of day care as it is generally experienced.

The Thomas Coram Research Unit (TCRU) project

This British longitudinal study (Hennessy *et al.*, 1990; Melhuish *et al.*, 1990; Melhuish, 1991) of day care began in 1982 and included 255 families with their first child. They all lived in the London area and about three-quarters of the mothers returned to full-time work before their child was nine months old; the others stayed at home with their child. The women who were returning to work intended to use one of three types of day care: a relative, a childminder or a private day nursery.

The children stayed in the project from birth until six years of age and during that time they were visited at home on four occasions: when they were four months old, eighteen months, three years and six years. Information was collected in a variety of ways including tests of language development and intelligence, observations of the child at home and in the day care setting, and questionnaires completed by mothers, caregivers and teachers. In addition to this information collected on the children at each visit, the mother was interviewed to gather information on her work pattern, her partner's work pattern and childcare arrangements. In this way it was possible to build up complete histories of the day care arrangements for each child in the project which included not only the changes that had taken place but the reasons for those changes.

The data collected were used to answer a number of questions about the development of the children. These included: Are there differences in the development of children in different types of day care? Does the length of time spent in day care affect the development of children? Do the number of changes in day care arrangements affect children's development?

This is one of the few British studies of young children in day care and, unlike many other studies, covered children in different types of care including relatives, who are not often studied. Because the researchers collected extensive information on the children and their parents before day care began (and subsequently on the day care experience of the children) it has been possible to look in some detail at the way in which children's day care experiences affect their development. However, the sample of women who took part in the project did not include representatives of all groups of women. When compared to a national sample there are more women in the project in professional and managerial jobs and fewer women in manual jobs. At the beginning of the project all children lived with both parents and the mothers were all born in Britain. The results, therefore, cannot be generalized to all children.

The FAST project

The FAST project is a major Swedish longitudinal project (Andersson, 1989, 1990) being carried out in the cities of Stockholm and Gothenburg, and one part of the project has involved a study of children in different types of day care. The children were three or four years old when they first took part in the project; two-thirds lived with two parents and one-third lived with one parent. Information on day care before the age at which the children entered the project was collected retrospectively and the rest of the project was longitudinal. When the children were eight years old and again when they were thirteen their development was assessed and their teachers completed questionnaires about their school work and social skills.

Children attended day care centres (day nurseries) or family day care (similar to childminders), or a combination of the two until they started school at age seven. About one-third of the children were under a year old when they first started in day care. The quality of day care in Sweden is very high. Staff in day nurseries are well trained to provide care and educational stimulation. There is usually one member of staff for every four or five young children (Andersson, 1989). Childminders are employed by their local authority and are encouraged to take part in training courses. A substitute is provided by the authority if the childminder is ill.

The data collected were used to answer the questions: Does age of starting day care have an effect on development? Does the type of day care affect development? The project is unusual in that it has information on the development of the children right up to the age of thirteen. Very few other studies go beyond the start of primary school. However, because day care in Sweden is of such high quality the results may not apply to other countries. In addition, because the children were not recruited to the project until they had been attending day care for some time it was not possible to say whether there were differences between the groups when they first started attending day care.

Howes' study of day care quality

This American study of day care quality (Howes, 1988) included eighty-seven children who attended a university nursery school. The children all began attending the nursery school when they were aged about three and a half but most had attended some type of day care before then. Information about the children's early day care experiences was collected retrospectively from the parents using a questionnaire. The children had attended either day nurseries or childminders and the researchers were able to obtain information on the quality of the care which the individual children received. A day care setting was rated as being of high quality if the caregiver(s) had some childcare training, the groups were small, there were fewer than eight children to each adult, there was an educational curriculum for each child and adequate physical space. When the children were about eight years old and were attending school their teachers completed questionnaires about their school work and their behaviour. In addition, parents completed a questionnaire about behaviour at home.

The questions asked of the data were: Does the age at which a child begins attending day care affect adjustment to school? Does the stability of day care arrangements affect adjustment to school? Does the quality of day care arrangements affect adjustment to school? Are there differences in school adjustment depending on whether day care was full time or part time?

The project was one of the first to identify the importance of the stability of day care arrangements. It also collected information on important aspects of day care quality. However, the researchers were only able to collect the information on quality in the day care arrangement which the child attended immediately before attending the university nursery school. The quality experienced by children whose day care arrangements changed many times may not be adequately measured by this method. The sample of families who took part in the project may also limit the extent to which the results can be generalized. The children came from a range of ethnic backgrounds and their parents varied in their levels of educational achievement but the fact that they all went to so much trouble to enrol their children in the school suggests that their commitment to education may have been above average.

The National Child Care Staffing Study

This American study of day care workers (Whitebook, Howes and Phillips, 1989) is unique among studies of day care because of its interest in the adults who work in day nurseries. The project was carried out in five cities in the USA in 1988. The aims of the project were to collect information on the background and job satisfaction of day care workers and to explore the ways in which day care workers contribute to the quality of day care settings. A total of 227 day nurseries were included in the project.

Each day nursery was visited by researchers from the project who gave it a rating using a measure of quality. The researchers also used a measure of teacher sensitivity to build up a more detailed picture of adult–child interaction. In every day nursery the director and six other members of staff were interviewed. The interviews were used to collect information on the background of the staff members, their experience of caring for children, work conditions, education, job satisfaction and recommendations for improving the childcare profession. In some of the day nurseries the development of the children was assessed. The researchers also studied the relationship between children and day care workers and asked the workers to rate certain aspects of the children's development.

The data collected by the researchers were used to answer questions about the relationship between caregivers' work environments (this included wages, benefits such as sick leave and reduced cost day care, paid holidays and in-service training) and the care provided for children: Does the quality of the work environment influence the quality of care provided for children? Does the work environment affect staff turnover? Does teacher behaviour affect children's development? Does staff turnover affect children's development?

The project has important implications for our understanding of day care and its impact on children because it found links between the working conditions of staff and the quality of care provided for children. These findings suggest that the development of children in day care is affected by conditions in which the carers must work. It is important to be cautious when deciding whether the results of research of this nature carried out in one country may be applied to another. However, there are similarities between day care organization in the USA and Britain (discussed in Chapter 1) which suggest that many of the relationships between work environment and day care environment may be relevant to Britain.

Day care and development

Having read the first three chapters the reader should have some appreciation of the complexity of the issues involved in the study of day care and children's development. Day care means different things in different countries and even in one country the experiences of children in day care may vary considerably. In contrast the researchers have been very consistent (or repetitive) in the questions which they have asked. Fortunately this situation is now changing with the increasing recognition of the complexity of the issues. In the next three chapters the emphasis is on describing the thinking, language and social development of children and discovering whether day care research has anything to offer to our understanding of how day care affects this development.

Summary

(1) Research can be used to test theories of child development, to provide a broad base of knowledge for decision-making and to supply information on how to improve services.
(2) Researchers' backgrounds and opinions will be reflected in the types of questions which they ask about day care.
(3) The design of a research project depends on the nature of the question it is supposed to answer and on the available time and resources.
(4) The results of a research project are relevant only to those families and children who are similar to the families and children who took part in the project.
(5) The emphasis of day care research is changing with an increasing acceptance of the complex interaction of day care and home environments in influencing child development.

Suggested further reading

Phoenix, A., Woollett, A. and Lloyd, E. (eds) (1991) *Motherhood: Meanings, Practices and Ideologies*, Sage, London.

Schaffer, H.R. (1990) *Making Decisions About Children*, Blackwell, Oxford.

4
THE DEVELOPMENT OF THINKING

This is the first of three chapters which present and discuss the findings of research relevant to the development of children in day care. Each of the chapters discusses a different aspect of child development. The first part of each chapter – 'The developing child' – describes the general course of child development and introduces some theories which explain why development should proceed in a particular way. The second part – 'The effects of day care' – introduces the findings of projects which have studied the development of children in day care.

This chapter deals with the development of thinking which is also called *cognitive* development. Thinking is a very complex process and in order to study and to understand the development of thinking it is sometimes divided into three component activities: perception, memory and concept formation. The first part of the chapter describes some of the changes that take place in these three activities during the first seven years of life and then describes a theory of cognitive development which suggests that these changes come about through children's interaction with the environment. The importance of the environment for cognitive development is again emphasized in the discussion of the results of day care studies in the second part of the chapter. The possibility that day care might compensate for a less stimulating home environment is investigated in one project. Other projects investigate the ways in which the caregiver, the quality of the day care environment and the stability of day care arrangements affect children's cognitive development.

Part one: The developing child

The development of perception

Consider a seven-year-old boy and his one-month-old baby sister sitting in the back of their parents' car, driving along a motorway. What do the two children see? The boy can see the back of two heads which he recognizes instantly as those of his parents. Outside he can see cars, lorries and buses some of which are travelling in the same direction and others going the opposite way. He can see some vehicles going slowly, which his car overtakes, and other vehicles going fast, which overtake him. By the side of the road he sees objects which he recognizes as buildings, walls and fences, trees, fields and farm animals. Now think about what his baby sister is taking in from her surroundings. She sees two round dark shapes in front of her; occasionally one of these moves and becomes something she does recognize, a smiling human face. Outside large numbers of different-coloured objects appear and disappear, some from behind and some from in front. Beyond these objects there is a blur of different shapes and colours. Sometimes everything is green with a few brown or black dots, other times there are large mainly brown rectangular objects visible.

Why do the two children see such different things? Firstly, the baby's visual system is less developed than her brother's so she is less able to take in fine detail, less able to see rapidly moving objects and less able to focus on distant objects. Secondly, her lack of experience or knowledge means that even when she can see things clearly, for example the back of her parents' heads, she may not recognize them. Her seven-year-old brother, however, has a fully developed visual system and is able to see everything as clearly as his parents. He is able to spend a long time looking at one thing and then to switch quickly to looking at something at a different distance. The difference between him and his parents is only one of experience. He may not be able to recognize the squiggles and shapes on the blue signs whereas they can effortlessly read the signposts; he may identify some buildings as houses and shops but may not be able to identify modern houses and old ones or distinguish between factories, warehouses and blocks of flats.

Perception refers to our ability to make sense of the information we receive from our senses. The description of the brother and sister in the car referred to their ability to see, or their visual perception, but we have four other senses apart from sight. These are hearing, touch, smell and taste. Through these senses the brain receives information from the moment we are born. Different sounds, sights, temperatures, tastes and feelings have to be interpreted. At first newborn babies seem very unresponsive to most of the stimuli around them but as they grow it becomes apparent they can distinguish between different sights and sounds (they recognize their mother's voice and face), different tastes and smells (they like some foods and not others), different surfaces (they like hard things to bite on and soft things to lie on) and so on. Sight and hearing appear to be most important for human development and it is these two aspects of perception that have been studied most.

Using the fact that babies will respond differently when they perceive something new and interesting, researchers have been able to find out a lot about babies' perception. For example, it is known that babies' ability to hear is very similar to that of adults though it appears that young babies require a higher volume to respond than adults or older children do. Babies only twelve hours old recognize their mother's voice which indicates very rapid learning (De Casper and Fifer, 1980), though of course some of this learning may have taken place while the baby was still in the uterus.

A lot has also been learned about the visual ability of babies. Newborn babies are unable to bring objects at different distances into focus. They only focus on objects about twenty-five centimetres away. This is roughly the distance from an adult's face if the baby is cradled in the adult's arms.

By four months, however, their focusing ability is near adult level. The ability of newborn babies to perceive patterns is very poor so that, for example, closely spaced black and white stripes are seen just as plain grey. By about six months, however, this ability is also at adult level. Young babies are more interested in external boundaries of shapes and objects than in their internal patterns. They show an increasing preference for complexity with increasing age.

Although the basic visual systems in the brain are working well before babies reach their first birthday, their perception does not reach adult levels for several more years. This is partly because their lack of knowledge does not allow them to make sense of all that they see, but it is also because other related abilities are still immature. In order to take in information it is important to concentrate or attend. Babies and young children are able to attend for a much shorter time than adults and this limits the amount of information they can perceive. They are more easily distracted by things going on around them. Some time between the ages of five and seven years children show dramatic changes in their ability to attend and concentrate and are thus able to understand more complex visual stimuli. This may be because at the same age children develop the ability to focus for longer periods and increase the speed at which they can change their focus from near to far objects.

In summary, research with babies indicates that at birth they are able to hear quite well but that their vision takes a few months to develop to adult levels. Research with both animals and humans indicates that improvements in visual perception are partly the result of changes which take place in the brain as it matures and partly as a result of visual experience.

The development of memory

Much of the information which reaches our brain through our senses is ignored or forgotten but much is stored in memory. Without the ability to remember we would know no more about the world than the newborn baby.

From the moment they are born babies can remember. We know this because babies respond differently to new sights and sounds than to those they have seen or heard before. In babies this ability is limited to recognizing very simple shapes or patterns and to very simple sounds (one syllable). As they get older they are able to recognize more complex patterns, such as faces, and complex sounds, like words. Six-year-olds are able to recognize pictures of simple objects almost as well as adults but experiments suggest that the ability to recognize complex scenes continues to improve beyond that age.

Older children and adults can also *recall* things even when they are not there. The ability to recall includes, for example, the ability to repeat a telephone number, to recount what you did last night or to recite a poem. Adults generally find these tasks more difficult than recognizing and there is evidence from many experiments to suggest that children develop the ability to recall only slowly during childhood.

Most psychologists agree that the memories of young children are less good than those of adults but opinions differ about why this is so. Some suggest that children do not have as much space available in their memory as adults and that this limits their ability. There is some evidence that this is true. If adults are asked to repeat a list of numbers or letters after hearing them just once they can usually remember about seven. Younger children remember fewer but as they get older the number gradually increases.

Other psychologists argue that more important than the difference in the size of available memory is the difference in the way adults and children use their memory. If adults are asked to remember something they usually use *strategies*. A strategy often used is *rehearsal*, that is repeating something over and over again. This can work well for learning a new phone number but more help is needed if something more complex is to be learned. Research has shown that adults asked to remember long lists of words will often organize them into related groups. This system of grouping or *chunking* seems to improve the memory. Children do not seem to use these strategies spontaneously but if they are taught them their ability to remember improves greatly.

In summary, research on memory has shown that even newborn babies can remember but at first this is limited to recognizing. As children get older they are able to recall things. The improvements in the ability to recall may be due to changes in the size of memory available, to differences in the way memory is used or to both. One result which all experiments confirm is that remembering something meaningful is much easier than remembering things which have no meaning. The ability to understand and to interpret in a meaningful way is linked to the way in which knowledge is organized within memory.

The development of concepts

In order to use the mass of information that comes into the brain and is stored in memory it is necessary to organize it in some way. This is achieved by grouping similar objects or ideas together to form *concepts*. Just as the ability to see and to remember improves as the child gets older so does the ability to form concepts. Newborn babies know nothing about the world but learning begins immediately and so too begins the process of trying to understand. Early attempts at understanding are limited because the baby knows little, but research suggests that babies soon begin to recognize similarities between objects. The first attempts to organize this knowledge are sometimes called *preconcepts*. Because babies cannot use language these preconcepts are linked to feelings and to the senses.

As babies get older they gain control of their arms and legs. This and the ability to see clearly improve the potential for developing more complex concepts. Objects can be grouped together according to their reactions to the babies' movements. For example, a preconcept of 'things which make noise when hit' might include some toys or the side of the cot but not a blanket or a teddy bear.

By two years children are developing language and for the first time concepts may have names. As more is learnt about the world, more concepts can be acquired and links can be made between them. For example the concepts of cat, dog and cow are learnt, then the three concepts are linked because they are part of a larger (or *superordinate*) concept called *animal*. Developing a complex system of concepts is dependent on having a stimulating environment which provides an opportunity for learning. The importance of opportunities for learning is discussed in detail in the next section.

A theoretical perspective

The Swiss psychologist Jean Piaget developed a comprehensive theory of human cognitive development that has been very influential. According to Piaget's theory children learn primarily through discovery rather than by direct teaching. It is therefore important to provide children with a stimulating environment which will encourage learning. Piaget also believed that children go through a number of stages of development characterized by increasingly complex ways of thinking and understanding the world. At each stage children should be given stimulation appropriate to their abilities but challenging enough to encourage further development. Although Piaget described four stages of development, only the first two will be discussed here as they are more relevant to the first seven years of life.

The stage from birth to about two years Piaget called the *sensori-motor stage*. At this stage babies learn through their senses and through moving about in their environment. Throughout most of the stage the child has limited language ability, and concepts (or preconcepts) are formed through the senses and by doing things. Two of the main tasks for children at this stage are to distinguish between themselves and the rest of the world and to learn that things in the outside world continue to exist even when they cannot be seen. Piaget called the latter process developing a concept of *object permanence*. Piaget believed that until about nine months of age babies lack this knowledge and without it their understanding of the world must be limited.

What environment will encourage learning during this stage of development? Because children are learning through their senses it is important to provide the opportunity to see and hear many different things. Before they can move around, children find mobiles interesting to look at because they change as they move. As babies develop control of their arms and legs it is important for them to have a chance to move freely. Interesting objects hung on a piece of string can be pushed and kicked and the effects can be watched. Babies also need to be given objects which can be picked up and moved around. Towards the end of the first year, as object permanence develops, babies enjoy hiding games with objects and adults.

Towards the end of the sensori-motor stage an important change in children's thinking occurs. They become capable of using symbols. The symbols of which we are most aware are words. As adults it is hard to imagine thinking without words and yet until the age of about two this is exactly what children must do. Once children begin to use language they are able to think in a very different way and they move on to the second stage of development.

The second stage of development Piaget called the *pre-operational stage*. This covers the ages from approximately two to seven years. Although children are now using language when they think, they still differ from adults in important ways. In particular, they are easily deceived by the appearance of things. This was demonstrated by Piaget using a number of well-known *conservation* experiments. In a typical conservation experiment a five-year-old is shown two identical lumps of plasticine and asked which is bigger. She states correctly that they are both the same size. The experimenter, in full view of the child, then makes one lump into a round ball and the other into a long thin snake. When asked again which one has more plasticine, the child is likely to say that the long piece has more. An adult might agree that the long piece of plasticine looks bigger but the adult also knows that nothing was added and nothing taken away so concludes that they must be the same size. The child also knows that nothing was added and nothing taken away but places more faith in the fact that one looks bigger.

Piaget also demonstrated that during the pre-operational stage of development children differ from adults in that they are more *egocentric*. This means they have difficulty seeing things from the point of view of other people. For example, a child may find it difficult to explain a story or an event coherently to another person because she assumes that the other person knows as much as she does.

Many of the things which children learn during the pre-operational stage form the foundation of later complex abilities such as mathematics and abstract thinking. If they are provided with sand, water, plasticine and other materials they can experiment with different shapes and amounts and will begin to learn about the physical properties of objects. Because children are now able to talk well, adults can help cognitive development by asking questions about what the children are doing and by asking about quantity (which has more?) and appearance (what does it look like?). Questions like these encourage children to think about the objects they are playing with. Other simple activities such as giving a bottle of milk to everyone in the group can help to develop skills which are important in understanding numbers. As children learn more about the world their concepts change. This can be encouraged by pointing out similarities which the child may not have noticed and by talking with them and asking questions.

Criticisms of Piaget's theory

In recent years many psychologists have questioned aspects of Piaget's theory. They have suggested that Piaget frequently underestimated the abilities of young children. In particular, it has been suggested that babies may develop object permanence much earlier than had previously been thought and that young children may be better at logical thinking than had been supposed. Tom Bower and his colleagues (Bower, Broughton and Moore, 1971) have shown that babies may develop object permanence earlier than Piaget suggested. They did this by using a measure of change in heart rate to see if the babies were surprised. Using this technique they found that babies were surprised if something which they could see being hidden then disappeared. This suggested that they believed that the object had continued to exist even though they could not see it. In addition, Margaret Donaldson (1978) with her co-workers in Edinburgh demonstrated that older children are capable of thinking logically if the tasks they are given are more meaningful to them.

Jean Piaget, Tom Bower and Margaret Donaldson were primarily interested in describing the ways in which children normally learn to think and to reason. Their theories were generally not concerned with the way in which children differ from one another in their use of these abilities. Such differences between children do exist and psychologists have frequently attempted to measure them.

Individual differences

Children and adults differ in their perceptual abilities, in their memory and in the complexity of the concepts which they form. As these three abilities contribute to processes such as reading, problem-solving and generating ideas it is not surprising that there are individual differences in the ability to carry out these complex processes. Individual children's cognitive ability is generally accepted as the result of the influence of two related factors. The first factor is ability inherited from parents. Just as physical features, such as eye colour, are inherited so too are cognitive abilities such as remembering and reasoning. Children obviously cannot inherit their parents' actual knowledge of the world but they inherit a potential ability. The second factor influencing cognitive development is the environment in which the child is brought up. An environment which provides children with lots of things to learn will encourage the development of memory, perception and concept formation. The effects of inherited ability and environment are strongly related to one another because it is generally the parents from whom a child inherits characteristics who have a large effect on the child's environment. We know that more intelligent adults tend to provide more stimulating environments for their children. This makes it very difficult to estimate which, if either, is more important.

Although children's inherited potential cannot be altered plenty can be done to ensure that they experience a stimulating environment that may help develop their full potential. A stimulating environment for a young baby is not the same as a stimulating environment for a toddler or an older child.

Measuring differences in cognitive development

Intelligence tests (also called IQ tests) require children to use their perceptual, memory and conceptual abilities. They were first developed at the beginning of this century to assess children's potential for school success and have continued to be used widely in the field of education. Today many different IQ tests exist but they generally include questions which test similar abilities, for example memory, problem-solving, recognizing patterns, understanding spatial relations. A child's ability is calculated by comparing the child's score (the number of right answers) with the scores of a large number of other children of the same age. A child who has a higher score than most children of her age is said to have an advanced level of development, while a child who has a score the same as most children of the same age has an average level of development.

IQ tests have been criticized for a number of reasons, many of which relate to the fact that they have been used to label individual children in the school system in ways that are not helpful for their future development. While research on day care generally has not used IQ tests to label individual children, a more significant criticism is the cultural bias of such tests. Most of the tests were developed by white, middle-class psychologists who use a particular way of asking questions that may not be familiar to children who do not share their background and culture. These children are immediately at a disadvantage just as an adult would be if asked a question in a foreign language. Researchers investigating the effects of day care on children's cognitive development need to use IQ tests with caution when comparing groups of children, because it would be easy to confuse the effects of different day care environments with different cultural backgrounds if the children were not all from the same culture. Despite these criticisms IQ tests are extensively used in day care research because they provide a quick way of looking at differences in the developmental level of groups of children.

Part two: The effects of day care

Day care as compensation

One aspect of the research on day care and cognitive development is that projects have been designed with the intention of compensating for children's home environments by providing day care which is stimulating. These projects first appeared in the USA in the 1960s as part of a plan to compensate for the effects of living in poverty. The underlying belief was that providing stimulating environments for the children of poor families would increase their chances of success in school and therefore increase success in education and employment.

The **Abecedarian project** was described in Chapter 3; the results relevant to cognitive development are discussed here. Half of the children in the project began attending high quality day nurseries before they were six months old; the other children either attended community day care or stayed at home with their mothers. From that age their cognitive development was assessed every six months until they were aged four and a half. In this way it was possible to compare the children who had special day care with those who had none and others who had different types of day care. The six-monthly measures of cognitive development showed that generally children attending the special day care did best on the tests, followed by the children attending community day care, while the children who stayed at home did least well. Despite the positive effects of day care all the children showed some drop in their cognitive ability from eighteen to twenty-four months. However, this drop was least for the children attending special day care. Researchers concluded that the high quality day nursery was successful at stimulating the development of very young children. When the children moved from day care into school the teachers thought the children who had attended the special day care were more advanced than the other children in the project.

Another project, similar in design to the **Abecedarian project**, investigated whether educating families about child development would enhance the effects of early day care, or whether family education on its own was sufficient to provide a more stimulating environment for young children living in poverty (Wasik *et al.*, 1990). The children were all recruited to the project before they were three months old and their cognitive development was tested every six months until they were about four and a half years old. The children who attended special day care and whose parents had special education did better than the other children. However, special education without day care did not help the children.

These two studies demonstrate that at least in the short term (to the early school years) stimulating day care can promote the cognitive development of children from poor backgrounds. Unfortunately such high quality day care is not routinely provided and therefore the results cannot be generalized. In the next sections the research discussed is of more relevance to the day care which most children can expect to receive.

Large sample studies

In contrast to the **Abecedarian project**, which involved only small numbers of children receiving very atypical day care, the next two studies involved very large numbers of children from diverse backgrounds. In both cases the way in which the researchers have approached their topic is based on a common assumption that *mothers*, rather than *parents*, have primary responsibility for the care of children. In both studies the researchers only provide information on the work patterns of the *mothers* and present the results in terms of the effects of *maternal* employment although it can be assumed that many of the children needed day care because *both* their parents worked outside the home. The real distinction, therefore, is not between children with working mothers and other children but between children who have one working parent and those who have two. This distinction should be borne in mind when reading about the results in which the researchers refer to 'children with working mothers' or 'maternal employment'.

Both studies were carried out in the USA. The first involved over 500 four-year-olds (Desai, Chase-Lansdale and Michael, 1989). Because so many children were included in the project it was not possible to collect detailed information on each child so a quick test of cognitive development was used. The researchers already had extensive information on the families of the children from a previous project. For example, they had information on the mothers' education, employment, marital status and intelligence. Overall there were no effects on the cognitive development of the children if their mothers were in paid employment. However, when a more detailed analysis was carried out they found that boys but not girls from high-income families with working mothers had poorer scores on the measure of cognitive development. Looking specifically at the work record of the mothers it was found that boys from high-income families, whose mothers worked outside the home during their first year, had the poorest level of cognitive ability. There was only one finding relevant to girls and that was positive. Girls whose mothers returned to work in their second year did better on the test of cognitive ability than girls whose mothers never returned to work.

The second project (Milne *et al.*, 1986) had information on over 15,000 children. Most of them were attending primary school but some were older (between fourteen and sixteen years). Again because of the very large number of children detailed information on their development was not collected but for every child they had information on their reading and maths ability. Because the sample was so large it was possible to look separately at the effects of maternal employment on black and white children and on children in one- and two-parent families.

The results of the project demonstrate that the effects of maternal employment may be very different depending on the race, age and family type of a particular child. Maternal employment was associated with lower scores in maths and reading for white children from two-parent families. There were no effects on the reading or maths ability of black children from two-parent families. The effects of maternal employment on children in one-parent families also depended on the race and age of the children. Black primary school children had higher scores on the reading and maths tests if their mothers were employed than if they were not. There were no differences in the scores of the white children from single-parent families. This did not hold true for the teenage black children: for them maternal employment was associated with lower reading ability.

The similarities in the design and focus of these two studies have already been discussed. The results are also similar in that they suggest that maternal employment (and by implication day care) may have negative effects on certain groups of children. One important aspect of the findings is the different effect which day care had depending on the gender, race and age of children as well as the type of family of which they were part. These findings highlight the need to be cautious when talking about the 'effect' of day care because any 'effects' are likely to be relevant to particular groups of children, with particular backgrounds and under specific circumstances.

The limited information which was collected by the two projects and which allowed them to study the development of such large numbers of children is also a limitation when it comes to interpreting the findings. The second project, in particular, had no information about the day care arrangements made for the children. We know that not all children with working mothers are cared for by people outside the immediate family. Some are cared for by their mothers while they work, others are cared for by their fathers, so no non-parental care need be involved. We also know that day care arrangements differ in type and quality, and studies like these give us no information that will help us to understand how such arrangements may influence children's development. For example, the results reported might not be due to day care itself, but to specific types of day care settings or to differences between families that are unrelated to day care.

Only studies collecting more detailed information about the home and day care environments of children can begin to understand these relationships.

Quality of environment

It was mentioned in Chapter 3 that measuring aspects of home and day care environment is a recent feature of day care research. Researchers differ in their approach to the task. Some choose to use a standardized measure of environment quality which usually provides an overall rating for quality based, for example, on the facilities available for the children. Such measures are available for use in family homes, the homes of child-minders and day nurseries. Other studies have opted to measure specific aspects of the child's environment and to relate them to child development. For example, studies have measured adult:child ratio and the amount which adults speak to children in their care and related them to aspects of child development.

In **Howes's** study of day care quality she was interested in whether the quality of the care which children received in their day care setting would predict their teachers' assessment of academic progress three years after entering school. She found that, for boys, academic skills were predicted by having attended high quality care. For both boys and girls good academic skills were predicted by experiencing stable care; in other words children who had fewer changes in their care arrangements were more likely to have better academic skills than children who had many changes. This is a factor which will be discussed again in relation to the results of the **TCRU project**.

A recent study of day care in Sweden (Broberg *et al.*, 1989) measured day care quality using a standardized instrument which provided an overall rating of day care quality. Researchers were also interested in the amount of stimulation available in the children's home environments and that too was measured with a standardized instrument. A total of 140 children took part in the project which began when they were between one and two years old. The children were seen on three occasions: immediately before they began attending day care, one year later and two years later. The results of the project indicated that the children's cognitive development was best predicted by the amount of stimulation available in their homes and that there were no observable effects for the type or quality of day care. The researchers believe that their results are partly due to the uniformly high standard of day care in Sweden. In other countries where there is a greater level of variability in the standard of care provided for young children an effect for quality might be expected.

The role of caregivers

A study of day care carried out in Chicago in the 1970s (Clarke-Stewart, 1987b) chose to study the development of children in a variety of different day care settings by looking at specific aspects of the environment and relating them to the children's development. The children were two or three years old at the start of the project and were observed in three different environments: at home, in their day care setting and in a research centre. The observations allowed the researchers to build up a detailed picture of how the children spent their time at home and in day care and of their ability to interact with familiar and unfamiliar people. In addition to the observations the parents took part in a detailed interview, used to gather information about family background and attitudes. The children were seen on two occasions, one year apart, and on each occasion standardized tests were used to measure their developmental level.

The results of the project are interesting because they provide a relatively detailed account of the way in which specific aspects of the behaviour of carers and the children's physical surroundings are related to development. The results show that children in home-based day care (this included children who were cared for in their own home by a nanny and children cared for by childminders) were more likely to have higher levels of cognitive development if the caregiver had a higher level of education, had more conversations with them, had more physical contact with them and read to them. There were also differences in the development of the children depending on the physical surroundings of the home. Children did better on the developmental tasks when the home was neat and orderly, was organized around activities and contained fewer adult-oriented decorations. The results for the children attending day care centres (this included both nursery schools and day nurseries) demonstrate that similar features of caregiver behaviour and physical surroundings are associated with more advanced levels of child development. In centres in which the workers were older, had been in the centre longer and had more training in child development the children had better scores on measures of cognitive development. Children had lower scores on the same measures if the workers were more directing, demanding and punishing. Children did best when given the freedom to learn, when the teacher read to them and encouraged them to play with materials on their own. With respect to the physical environment of the day care setting, the children did best when the environment was safe and orderly and contained a variety of stimulating toys and educational materials.

Although these results are very interesting and appear to be consistent with widely held views that environments which are more stimulating will encourage children's cognitive development they must also be interpreted with caution. Because children in day care environments with certain characteristics tend to do better than children in day care environments without these characteristics it cannot be assumed that the environments have caused the differences in the children. The results of a Canadian study (Goelman and Pence, 1988) of children in different types of day care of varying quality showed that children who came from stimulating home environments in general went to stimulating day care environments and vice versa. The researchers refer to this phenomenon as some children having the best of both worlds and other children having the worst of both worlds. If this was the case in the project in Chicago then at least some of the differences thought to be the result of experiences in day care might be the results of experiences at home.

A second study of children (all eighteen months old) in day nurseries and at home focused on just one aspect of children's cognitive development – their level of play (Rubenstein and Howes, 1979). The researchers in the project observed small groups of children in day care and at home. They found that the way in which the children in day nurseries played was more advanced than the way in which the children at home played. The authors suggest that children play in a more advanced way when they are playing with other children than when they are playing alone. The reason why the children in the nurseries appeared to be more advanced was because they had more children of their own age available to play with. When the children at home were observed playing with a friend of their own age they did just as well as the children in nurseries. The results also showed that the behaviour of the adults was related to the level of play shown by the children. Mothers and caregivers whose emotional responses to the children were positive (including smiling at them, holding/hugging them, praising them and playing with them) had children who were more competent at play. In contrast to this, in homes and nurseries, if the children's behaviour was restricted and controlled then the children generally had lower levels of play.

These two studies which looked at specific aspects of children's environment both at home and in day care found that the behaviour of caregivers (including mothers) seemed to be related to the behaviour of children. Such studies cannot establish what causes the observed behaviour but at the very least they provide an interesting basis for future research.

Day care stability

The studies discussed in this chapter have looked at the effects of different aspects of the day care and home environment on children's cognitive development. The children attended group-based day care or day care in family homes with caregivers who provided them with more or less stimulation, and in some cases differences in cognitive development were found to be associated with these different arrangements. These studies, however, do not take into account the changes that individual children experience over time in their day care arrangements. This issue of day care history was introduced in Chapter 1. Chapter 2 provided some examples of the changes experienced by young children. With the emphasis of research changing there has been more interest in individual children's experiences and how these affect their life in day care.

The **TCRU project** collected information on the day care histories of children from birth to six years. The results showed that changes in day care were regularly experienced by the children during their first three years. More important was the finding that children who experienced more changes in their day care arrangements had a slower rate of cognitive development over the first three years. These children did not fall further behind from three to six years but neither did they catch up with the children with fewer changes. From the information collected it was possible to check whether the changes in day care arrangements were due to major changes in family life such as those brought about by the arrival of a new baby or the divorce of parents. The results suggest that they were not. However, the number of changes was related to mother's education level such that the children with the greater number of changes had the most educated mothers. In other circumstances these are the children who would be expected to have more advanced levels of development.

These results are very similar to those already reported by Carollee **Howes**. The results of her project were analysed separately for boys and girls; in both cases teachers' reports of academic skills were related to the stability of day care arrangements in the preschool period. Higher levels of academic skills were reported for children who had had more stable day care arrangements. Further confirmation is provided by the results of the **National Child Care Staffing Study** which found that children in day nurseries with higher staff turnover had lower levels of cognitive ability than children in day nurseries with more stable staffing.

These findings do not mean that changes in day care arrangements inevitably cause poorer cognitive development. The results are sufficiently striking, however, to suggest that researchers should consider further the reasons for changes in day care arrangements, how children cope with changes, and ways to minimize unnecessary change and to ease changes that are unavoidable.

Summary of day care research

(1) A stimulating day care environment experienced in the first years of life enhances the cognitive development of children from poor backgrounds.
(2) Studies involving large numbers of children from different backgrounds have found that the effects of day care differ depending on children's gender, race and age and type of family.
(3) High quality day care, as measured by specific aspects of the day care environment, appears to have a positive effect on children's cognitive skills.
(4) There is some evidence that children in day care environments which are orderly and organized and which have appropriate materials are more advanced in their cognitive development than children in other environments.
(5) There is some evidence that children whose caregivers are responsive to them, and who are less demanding and punishing, are more likely to have advanced cognitive development.
(6) Children in stable day care arrangements are more likely to have advanced cognitive development than children in unstable arrangements.

Suggested further reading

Donaldson, M. (1978) *Children's Minds*, Fontana, London.

5
LEARNING TO TALK

By the time children start school they are competent talkers. They have a large vocabulary of several thousand words, they talk grammatically and can understand and be understood by everyone. Yet at birth babies have just one means of communicating – crying. In the years which follow they must learn a highly complex system of communication and yet almost all children succeed with apparent ease. How does this happen and how important are adults in ensuring that children successfully complete this learning process? These questions are discussed in the first part of the chapter. The second part of the chapter discusses the findings of research projects which have studied the language development of children in day care. Studies have been chosen which emphasize the role of the caregiver in promoting language development.

Part one: The developing child

The first few months

Within the first few seconds of life babies cry and thus make their first act of communication. They are letting the world know that they are alive and well and that their lungs are functioning properly. In the next few weeks babies use crying as their principal form of communication and sensitive adults involved in the care of babies will quickly come to recognize that different cries signify different things. The main feelings that babies need to express are hunger, pain or discomfort, and boredom, and research has shown that there are indeed different types of cry associated with these. For example, a hunger cry starts quietly and intermittently and gradually increases in volume and frequency. A cry of pain, however, is usually loud from the start followed by a silence and then short gasping sounds.

Although babies can make a very limited range of sounds there is evidence that they are able to distinguish a much larger number. Using the fact that babies respond differently when they perceive something new (already described in Chapter 4) researchers have found that babies of only one month old can distinguish quite small differences in sound. When a recording of a voice saying 'pah' was played babies would stop sucking for a short while and then as they became used to the sound would start to suck again (Trehub and Rabinovitch, 1972). However, when 'pah' was changed to 'bah' babies stopped sucking again, indicating that they could hear the difference between the two sounds even though they could not produce them.

By the time babies are four or five weeks old a new sound is added to their vocabularies. They start to produce cooing sounds to express pleasure or contentment. At about the same time babies first start to smile and these two behaviours encourage caretakers to have 'conversations' with them. It is thought that these early 'conversations' are very important to later language development. Through them babies learn how to take turns and to concentrate on the speaker. An example of a 'conversation' between an adult and a baby of about six months old while the baby is having its nappy changed is given below.

Baby (waving arms and grimacing)
Adult Oh you don't like that do you?
Baby Oooo
Adult Yes that's better isn't it?
Baby (smiles)
Adult What a lovely smile. I thought that would be better
Baby Oooo

Babies of six months have learnt new ways of expressing themselves. Smiling, laughing, wriggling with excitement or pleasure, cooing, gazing and early forms of reaching or pointing are all ways that they can show adults that they are responding to their environment. The sensitive adult will respond to these early attempts to communicate in ways similar to those illustrated in the example above. Peek-a-boo and hiding games encourage babies to join in turn-taking and enjoy joint activity with other people. These experiences also help the baby to acquire a basic principle which underlies later communication and language development. That is, what they do affects what others do.

The second half of the first year

At about six months babies acquire a whole new range of sounds which they string together in complex combinations referred to as *babbling*. These sounds are often remarkably similar to adult speech in intonation and phrasing. It is interesting that babies in all countries babble using the same sounds despite the fact that the languages which they hear spoken vary in their sound patterns. Towards the end of the first year babbling changes and becomes restricted to the sounds of the language which a baby usually hears.

By nine or ten months babies have also developed more effective ways of communicating with adults. They have become adept at combining gestures or facial expressions with sounds to produce quite complex messages. For example, a baby in a high chair may point and shout angrily at a drink indicating that she wants that drink and wants it now! Later the same baby may wriggle excitedly, smile and lift her arms in the air to show her pleasure at the arrival of her father and that she wants him to pick her up.

Although babies of this age have become good communicators even without the use of language, they are even better at understanding other people. For example, the baby in the high chair excited by the arrival of her father will show that pleasure several minutes earlier if the person with her tells her that Daddy is about to come in. She does not need the physical presence of her father to feel pleasure, but can understand something about Daddy from the words 'There's Daddy coming in'. Similarly babies can follow simple instructions such as 'Give it to Granny' or 'Sit down'.

Early verbal stage

Between approximately nine and eighteen months children produce their first word (the average age is just over twelve months). First words are very exciting but they are also quite easy to miss as they are often very individual and may need translating by an adult who knows the child well. A sound is recognized as a word when it is regularly used to refer to the same object. Research on children's first words suggests that they are sometimes used to refer to objects or people only in certain situations. For example, a child might say 'teddy' only when she throws her teddy bear out of her cot and not when she wants her teddy or sees another teddy bear. Having used the word in this way for a few months the child will eventually go on to use the word 'teddy' in a whole variety of different situations and to apply it not only to her own teddy but to all teddy bears.

Children use their first words in other characteristic ways. For example, one child always said 'gog' when she saw a dog. At first she only said 'gog' to large dogs but she gradually increased her use of the word to include all dogs, large and small, and pictures of dogs in books and on television. Although 'gog' is not in the English language, this girl was using it correctly as a word and had started to talk. The next stage this child went through with her use of the word 'gog' was to use it for any hairy four-legged animal. If she saw a cat or a sheep she would still call it 'gog'. This very common process is called *overextension* and many examples can be found in children's early language.

Children also make the mistake of using a word to refer to too few things. For example, a child may learn to say 'ball' only to refer to her small blue ball but not to her sister's red ball or to any other ball that she sees. Using words in this way is called *underextension*.

Another important way in which first words are used is as *holophrases*. This means that although only one word is produced, the context and tone in which it is spoken can indicate a complete sentence. A child may look at her cup on the table and say 'allgone'. This may be a response to her mother's question 'Have you drunk your milk?'; it may be spoken loudly and angrily to indicate that she is thirsty and wants something to drink; it may be a question – 'Has my cup got anything in it?'; or it may be said with satisfaction to inform someone that she has enjoyed her drink and that now it is all gone. Once again this is a case in which a sensitive adult can help the child's language development. By listening to the tone and knowing the context the adult will be able to respond appropriately and the child learns that her attempts to talk are worthwhile.

Single words are typically learnt rather slowly and children often take several months to build up a vocabulary of twenty or so words. The next stage is for children to combine two or more words to make simple sentences. Some children learn a large vocabulary of single words before they combine any, others will start to combine words when they only have a few words in their vocabulary. Word combinations need some explanation. 'Allgone' as used by the child in the earlier example is not a word combination because the child has made it into one word and is not able to use the two parts independently. However, if the child went on to use phrases such as 'Daddy gone' or 'car gone' where 'gone' is being used independently with a number of other words then she has reached the stage of making simple sentences.

These early sentences are often referred to as *telegraphic speech*. In the same way as senders of telegrams omit all unnecessary words young children restrict their speech to bare essentials. To say 'I want to put the teddy in Mummy's bed' a child may say 'Teddy Mummy's bed'. Only the nouns

have been included; all pronouns, verbs and prepositions have been excluded. However, the word order is correct and children are starting to demonstrate their knowledge of grammar when they combine words in the right grammatical order. This early evidence of an understanding of grammatical rules is found in children learning all languages throughout the world. Once again, however, for the adult to know exactly what a child is saying she will have to be aware of the tone and context. To know whether 'Teddy Mummy's bed' means 'The teddy is in Mummy's bed', 'You put the teddy in Mummy's bed' or 'I want to put the teddy in Mummy's bed' will depend on watching the child for the accompanying gestures and listening to the tone that is used.

Although children just learning to talk may only be able to put together two or three words they are capable of following and understanding quite complex sentences. In the **TCRU project**, for example, eighteen-month-old children were asked to do various tasks as part of the assessment of their language and cognitive development. They were asked to point to a number of familiar objects on a page of black and white pictures (dog, house, shoe, car and so on), they were given a doll and asked to put it on a chair and then given a toy cup and told to give the doll a drink and then wipe its face. These were all tasks done with an unfamiliar adult and using unfamiliar toys but most of the children could complete most of the tasks. Although they would not have been able to use such complex language themselves they were able to understand it.

Later language development

By the time they reach their second birthday most children are using language routinely to communicate with other people. At times of stress they will still revert to non-verbal methods of expressing themselves. They may still frequently cry, shout, scream or become very withdrawn and maybe suck their thumbs or rock rhythmically. However, they are learning to use language in a wide variety of situations. They can ask for information ('Where my shoes?') and give information ('Water hot') and they can talk in simple terms about what has happened in the past ('Granny gone bus') and what might happen in the future ('Go swimming soon'). They can also use words for pretend play and to socialize with other children ('I'm Mummy and you're Daddy and here's our house') though this sort of co-operative play does not generally appear until some time after the third birthday. They are also using language to express their own personalities and assert themselves ('That's mine', 'Don't like milk', 'Give Mummy kiss').

From soon after the appearance of the first sentences children start to make *virtuous errors* in their speech. These are important because they show that they have learnt some grammatical rules and are trying to apply them. Children who have quite correctly been saying 'We went on the bus' may begin to say 'We goed on the bus'. They have learnt that the past tense usually takes 'ed' as an ending but have not yet learnt that there are valid exceptions to this rule. Another common virtuous error is in the misuse of 's' for plurals. 'Sheeps', 'childs' and 'moneys' are examples of this sort of mistake.

Many other mistakes in children's speech are common as they try out new words and expressions. These mistakes can often be very amusing but it is important for the adults around the children not to make fun of them. The most effective way of correcting them seems to be to repeat what the child has said using a correct version. 'My Daddy catched lots of mouses' could be corrected by saying 'Your Daddy caught lots of mice, did he? And what did he do with them?' In this way children gradually learn the exceptions to the rules of grammar and by the time they start school are talking fluently and confidently.

A theoretical perspective

Theories of language development aim to explain how children learn to use language to communicate effectively with other people. Many such theories exist and in general they emphasize either the role played by genetics or the role played by the environment. In this section one theory will be described which emphasizes the role of the environment, particularly the social context in which language is learnt.

When language is considered as a means of interacting with other people it becomes clear that children are learning skills that are important for communicating long before they have learnt any words. The 'conversation' between mother and baby described at the beginning of the chapter is an example of the *turn-taking* that takes place before a child learns to speak. These social situations mimic adult conversations in so far as each person's action is followed by an action from the other person just as people say things to one another in conversation. Early turn-taking games are dependent on the ability of adults to take turns, because babies have not yet acquired the skill.

Once children have learnt a basic skill such as turn-taking, how are they going to begin to make sense of the complex language they hear around them? Research on adults talking to children has shown that the child's task is made considerably easier by the fact that adults speak to children in a special way (Snow, 1977). This way of talking has been called *motherese* although it is not used exclusively by mothers but by other adults and by children as young as four years. Speech is modified in various ways such as using a higher pitch, shorter sentences and putting greater emphasis on the key words. This may attract attention to what the adult is saying and help to focus attention on the important words.

When children start to use simple sentences adults often *expand* the sentences by using the more complex conventional form. For example, if a child says 'Cake gone' the adult may expand the statement by saying 'The cake has all gone' so that the child gradually learns to make more complex and grammatical sentences. Alternatively the adult might *recast* the sentence by saying 'We've eaten up all the cake'. Recasting differs from expanding in that the topic of the child's sentence is used but talked about in a new way. Thus, children seem to be guided through the early stages of language development by the adults around them.

Proving that a special way of talking to children causes them to develop language more quickly and to have a more advanced level of verbal ability is very difficult. However, there is evidence that children are more attentive to simplified speech and if they listen they are more likely to learn. There is also evidence that children's language development is encouraged if the length of sentence that the adult uses is just slightly longer than the child's and if the adult tends to recast sentences.

Individual differences

Although children will all go through the stages described above they will do so at their own pace. One child will say her first word at nine months, another child at thirteen months. One child will learn lots of words very quickly, another will learn new words slowly. Although almost all children will eventually learn to use language to communicate, we also know that some will be more skilful at using language than others. Some will grow up to be able to express themselves clearly when talking to someone or when writing letters, others will find this much more difficult. Just as the pace of language development differs so does the older child's verbal ability.

In the last chapter individual differences in cognitive development were said to be the result of the child's inherited abilities and of the environment. This is also true of language development and verbal ability. Children's language development is partly the result of the abilities inherited from parents and partly the result of the environment in which they grow up and live.

Measuring individual differences

Chapter 4 described IQ tests and how they are used to measure differences in cognitive development. Standardized measures of language development are constructed in the same way. Children's knowledge of words or ability to make sentences are compared with the ability of children of the same age. If they know more words or are better at combining them than most other children of the same age then their language development is said to be advanced. If their abilities are less than those of other children then their language development is said to be slow.

There is much overlap between IQ tests and language assessments. Most IQ tests include items which measure children's verbal ability such as the ability to understand instructions, the ability to name pictures or the ability to define words. Many of the projects which are discussed in the second half of this chapter used tasks like these to measure language development and verbal ability.

Part two: The effects of day care

The role of caregivers

In comparison with the number of projects which have studied the effects of day care on cognitive development fewer have concentrated on language development. However, many of these have provided a detailed account of the way in which the day care environment and the behaviour of the caregiver influence language development.

One of the first studies of the language development of children in day care was conducted in Bermuda (McCartney, 1984) and involved children attending day nurseries. A total of 166 children between the ages of three and six years took part in the project. The researchers collected information on the quality of the day nurseries which the children were attending and were particularly interested in the extent and type of language used by caregivers. They observed children in each nursery to record how often caregivers and other children spoke to them. To discover to what extent differences in language ability were due to differences in home environments detailed information was collected from the parents on their age, education and occupation. The results of the project showed that, over and above the influence of the home, children in better quality day nurseries did better on the standard tests of language development. The researchers were also able to look in more detail at the ways in which the caregivers' speech was related to the children's language development. They found that in nurseries where the caregivers spoke to the children more often the children's language was more advanced. They also found that the manner of the caregivers' interaction was associated with the children's language development. Children in nurseries where they were usually spoken to as a means of controlling their behaviour did not do as well as children in nurseries where language was usually used as a means of exchanging information between adult and child.

Recent studies in three different countries (Britain, Canada and the USA) confirm these findings. When the children in the **TCRU project** were eighteen months old researchers visited them in their nursery or at the home of their childminder or relative. Children who were not in day care were visited at home. Each visit lasted for one hour and during that time the researchers made detailed observations of the children at play (routine activities such as meals and story times were avoided). The observations focused on the children's activities and on anyone who interacted with the children. In this way the researchers were able to describe the experiences of the children in the different day care settings. Because the mothers had been interviewed, the length of time the children were spending in day care was known as well as detailed information about other aspects of their family background.

The second aspect of the project involved collecting information on the children's language development. Mothers were asked to keep a diary in which they recorded everything their child had said during one week. At eighteen months most children have a small vocabulary and are only combining words in very short sentences so most mothers could complete the diaries without too much difficulty. Children were rated as more advanced in their language development if they knew more words and were better at combining words to make simple sentences.

The researchers were interested in which aspects of the children's home or day care environment would predict their level of language development. They found that girls were more likely to be advanced at combining words than boys. They also found that children who were in environments where they were spoken to more often and environments with responsive caregivers were more likely to be advanced at combining words than children who were in environments where they were not spoken to often or environments with less responsive caregivers. A responsive caregiver is one who is likely to respond to a child's attempts to communicate. The observations revealed that, in the **TCRU project**, the children in the day nurseries were less likely to be spoken to than children at home or the children in other types of day care. These children were also less likely to get a response to their attempts at communication than were children being cared for at home or in the home of a relative.

A second project, carried out in Canada (Goelman and Pence, 1987, 1988), had results very similar to the **TCRU project**. The project involved sixty children between three and five years old who were all attending childminders. The children were video-recorded during a play activity in their own homes and in homes of their childminders. The videos were then transcribed so that specific aspects of the activities of the children and the adults could be looked at in more detail. The children's language development was assessed using standardized tests which measured their ability to name pictures and to express themselves. Children were more likely to have advanced language development if they were spoken to more often when with their childminder. They were also more likely to have advanced language development if adults had conversations with them rather than simply telling the children what to do.

Two American studies report findings consistent with those just discussed. A project involving a small group of eighteen-month-old children (Rubenstein and Howes, 1979) found that children cared for at home and those in day care were affected by the way adults spoke to them. The children were more likely to speak to the adults (both mothers and caregivers) if the adults responded to them and if the adult recast or expanded the children's sentences. The **National Child Care Staffing Study** found that children's language development was more likely to be advanced if caregivers responded to children's speech and if the caregivers were more sensitive to their needs.

These studies on language development are remarkably consistent in their findings despite the fact that they were carried out in four different countries. The studies included children cared for at home with their mothers, in day nurseries and in the homes of childminders and yet they are all in agreement on the types of adult behaviour which encourage language development. Children tended to do better on measures of language development if they had conversations with adults, if they were spoken to more often, if their sentences were recast or expanded and if adults were responsive to them.

Many factors might influence the way in which adults respond to children. For example, an adult looking after a large number of children will not have the opportunity to respond to them individually as successfully as an adult with a small number of children. An adult who knows a young child may be better at understanding what the child is trying to communicate because children's first words are sometimes idiosyncratic. If children are cared for in an environment with many new caregivers then none of the caregivers may get a chance to understand the children's first words. In the case of the **TCRU project** it is not possible to say exactly why the day nursery environments were less responsive but we do know that adults were responsible for larger numbers of children in the day nurseries than in any of the other types of day care.

Verbal ability

The projects discussed so far in this chapter have studied the language development of young children who are still in day care. Other projects have assessed the verbal ability of school-age children who had previously attended day care, to study the long-term effects of day care experiences.

The **FAST project** in Sweden collected information on the verbal ability of the children in the project when they were eight years old. The results showed positive effects of early day care attendance. Children who had attended day care before they were a year old performed better on the tests of verbal ability than children who began attending when they were older or who had never attended. Children who began attending day care as toddlers did better than children who were older when they started. The researchers did not measure the quality of the day care environments but it has already been mentioned that day care in Sweden is of high quality and this factor probably contributed to the advanced development of the children who started attending earlier.

Because the **TCRU project** followed the development of children from birth to six years old it has results relevant to both language development and subsequent verbal ability. The results relevant to language development have already been discussed. Information on verbal ability was collected when the children were six years old. Standardized tests were administered which measured the ability to name pictures (naming vocabulary) and the ability to define words. The results showed that children did least well on the measure of vocabulary if they had attended day care settings where there were fewer communications with the children and where caregivers were less responsive to the children's attempts to communicate. It was mentioned in the section discussing language acquisition that at eighteen months children in day nurseries generally experienced this poorer type of language environment. Visits to the day care settings when the children were three years old confirmed that in some of the day nurseries they were still experiencing unresponsive language environments. This may have contributed to their performance on the vocabulary task at six years but it is important to note that all children performed equally well on a task to define words which may be a more advanced measure of verbal ability.

Unfortunately most of the studies of day care and verbal ability do not have the detailed information on the environment collected by the studies described in the previous section. The results are therefore more difficult to interpret. The **FAST project** reported positive effects of attending day care. The **TCRU project** reported on the language environments of the children in different day care settings and found that day care in which caregivers were not responsive to the children had a negative effect on one aspect of verbal ability. Because the negative finding was limited to one measure of verbal ability it is difficult to say how important this result is. If the effects of day care on later language ability are to be fully understood, however, more studies will have to look in detail at the language environment of day care and children's verbal ability as they get older.

Day care as compensation

In Chapter 4 the results of the **Abecedarian project** were discussed in relation to cognitive development. The researchers also collected information on verbal ability when the children were in their first and second years in school. At the end of the first year there were no differences between the ability of the children who had attended the special day care and those who had not. At the end of the second year the children who had attended special day care were reported to have more advanced verbal ability than the children who had not attended. The special day care was designed to be very stimulating and it is likely that the caregivers responded to the children in the ways described in the section on day care and language development thus promoting their language development.

Summary of day care research

(1) There is substantial evidence that children's language is more advanced in day care environments where they are spoken to more often and in which caregivers are more responsive to their attempts to communicate.
(2) There is some evidence that day care environments, particularly those of high quality, are associated with more advanced verbal ability in older children and that unresponsive environments are associated with less advanced verbal ability.
(3) A very stimulating day care environment experienced in the first years of life enhances the language development of children from poor backgrounds.

Suggested further reading

Tizard, B. and Hughes, M. (1984) *Young Children Learning*, Fontana, London.

6

THE DEVELOPMENT OF SOCIAL AND EMOTIONAL BEHAVIOUR

This chapter describes some of the main changes which take place in the children's ability to interact with other people and to develop emotional maturity. The second part of the chapter discusses the research on the social and emotional development of children in day care. Some aspects of social and emotional development have received more attention from researchers than others. Most noticeable has been the amount of research on the attachment relationships formed by children who begin attending day care early in their first year. However, attachment is only one aspect of the children's developing ability to relate to other people. This chapter will also discuss the importance of children's friendships, children's developing awareness of other people, their positive interactions with them and the common types of problem behaviour that are exhibited by many children.

Part one: The developing child

Relationships

The information on the cognitive and language development of newborn babies should have convinced the reader that it is important for babies to develop social relationships with adults who will take care of their needs. Despite their helplessness, newborn babies have some instinctive behaviours which help them to develop these relationships. Firstly, they bring to every social situation the ability to learn. In Chapter 4 it was mentioned that babies very quickly learn to recognize their mother's voice, they also quickly learn to recognize the sounds that precede feeding. Later they learn more complex things like how to attract someone's attention by crying. As well as this general ability to learn, all newborn babies have specific abilities that help them to interact with other people. For example, a human face contains a mixture of patterns likely to attract the attention of babies and human speech is more likely to be of interest to babies than most other sounds. Secondly, babies have behaviour patterns of their own that are likely to produce a response from other people. Among these are crying and smiling. Crying may result in being picked up, and smiling usually provokes a smile from any watching adult. Thus, babies quickly learn that some of their actions produce responses from other people.

Thirdly, from an early age babies enjoy someone responding to their actions. Responding in this way is called *contingent responding* and is dependent on the sensitivity of the adult. The adult must wait until the child has finished an action and then make some response. The response might be a comment on what the child has done or may be an imitation of the child's own action. From a very early age children enjoy engaging in these activities and this helps to encourage contact with adults.

The earliest relationships

During the first year of life one important aspect of children's social development is learning to form relationships with other people. Newborn babies do not seem to show a preference for particular people and when they first begin to smile the smiles are directed towards anyone. But this behaviour changes as they get older and by the time they are five to seven months old there is a very obvious change. For the first time babies seem to prefer familiar people. This preference may take the form of smiling more at those people or being more easily consoled by them when hurt or upset. By about nine months, when most babies are able to move about by crawling, they will follow or try to follow the people they prefer or will regularly look to see whether they are near by. They will usually cry or show some sign of upset if the preferred person leaves the room or disappears from sight. At about the same age many babies develop a fear of strangers. Babies who were previously happy to meet new people will become wary of them and may even become upset if the unfamiliar person approaches them.

In the early 1950s John Bowlby (1971, 1975) developed a theory about the importance of the child's early relationships. In particular he concentrated on the relationship between mother and baby. The word which he used to describe that relationship was *attachment.* He chose the word because he believed that children wanted to be physically close to their mothers and would become upset if this were not possible. Babies who cannot move by themselves can only attract attention by crying and because adults find crying distressing they will usually act quickly to calm the child. Bowlby interpreted this crying as a way of reassuring children of their mothers' presence. Bowlby proposed that it was important for mothers to provide their children with that closeness because only then would children learn to be secure in their relationships. When children's needs for closeness, food, comfort or stimulation are satisfied by their mothers then the relationship between them becomes *secure*, meaning that the children are confident of being cared for. When children's needs are regularly not satisfied they develop the expectation that they will not be cared for and the relationships which develop are *insecure*.

But Bowlby's theory went further than considering the security or insecurity of babies' relationships. He suggested that the relationships developed as babies are important because they affect future development. This conclusion is controversial and the studies carried out over the last decade have produced contradictory findings. For example, some studies have reported that babies who are insecurely attached are less likely to be as psychologically healthy as children who are securely attached (Arend, Gove and Sroufe, 1979; Sroufe, Fox and Pancake, 1983) Other studies find no differences between securely and insecurely attached infants as they get older.

Bowlby developed his theory as a result of research on children who were reared in residential institutions or who were separated from their parents because they had to spend a long time in hospital. Research on these children showed that they were more anxious and clinging than most children, that they were more afraid of strangers and that they were more likely to develop problem behaviour as they got older. Additional support for his theory came from research on animals which showed that young raised without mothers had later social problems.

The theory had the effect of drawing people's attention to babies' needs for warm, loving relationships. The other effect was to focus very specifically on the relationship between mothers and babies to the exclusion of the babies' relationships with other people. Although most people now acknowledge the need for babies to develop strong relationships there has been a lot of discussion about whether the relationships must be with the mothers and whether babies are capable of forming strong attachment relationships with a number of adults.

Criticisms of attachment theory

Like other theories attachment theory is not accepted by all researchers in psychology. One criticism of the theory is that it is based on the assumption that being securely attached is somehow normal and necessary for healthy development. Although about two-thirds of children in the USA are securely attached (little research on attachment has been carried out in Britain but the figures seem to be about the same), research evidence from other countries such as Japan and Germany shows great variation in the proportion of children with secure attachments. It seems likely, therefore, that different child-rearing practices are associated with differences in attachment relationships.

Secondly, attachment theory has been criticized because much of the early work concentrated on the relationship between mother and child. Research evidence suggests that mothers are not necessarily the only or the main attachment figure for most children. In Britain, research from the 1960s (Schaffer and Emerson, 1964) suggested that as many as one-third of children seemed to have their strongest attachment to someone other than their mother. Unfortunately, this fact was ignored by many researchers who continued to concentrate on the mother–child relationship and to ignore other relationships.

Thirdly, there has been criticism of the way in which the attachment relationships are measured. There is a standard procedure in which the mother and child are observed called the *strange situation*. It was designed as a mildly stressful situation for children which would encourage attachment behaviours, for example looking for comfort from the mother or seeking contact with her. The procedure involves observing the reactions of children to a fixed series of mildly stressful events which include being separated from their mothers, meeting a stranger and being reunited with their mothers after a few minutes' separation. Children who seek comfort from their mothers and who are consoled by their mothers' presence are classified as *securely attached*. The procedure has been criticized because it bears very little resemblance to the type of everyday interaction between mothers and children.

Making friends

While children are developing close relationships with a few people who are important in their lives they are also meeting other adults and children. These may be brief encounters in parks or playgrounds or longer contacts with family friends. It appears that from about twelve to eighteen months children are very interested in one another. Observing toddlers in a playground quickly demonstrates that they spend a lot of time looking at one another with interest. At this early age, however, children are not very skilled at interacting with one another and the initial interest may never progress beyond staring. As children get older they learn how to play with other children and how to make friends. The abilities needed when meeting new people or when joining a group are sometimes called *social skills*.

Researchers have described the changes that take place in the ways in which children interact with one another as they get older (Parten, 1932). Early behaviour is quite often categorized as *solitary play* which implies that the child is playing alone even though other children are present; however, the child may display an interest in what is going on by looking at what the others are doing. *Parallel play* describes the situation that is often seen in the behaviour of children in a sand pit, where the children are all very close to one another and are playing very similar games but are not yet interacting with one another. Once social skills develop children begin to take part in more *interactive play*. This means that children are not only close to one another but are also sharing and co-operating. A good example of this type of activity is building a lego model together or making a sand-castle on the beach. Children of all ages play alone or play in parallel with other children but researchers have found that these types of behaviours are much more common in younger children. By the time children are six or seven they are likely to engage in a lot of interactive play and about this time group games with rules begin to become a feature of their play.

How important are friends?

Unfortunately very little research has been done on the importance of the friendships made by preschool children. One project in the USA (Field, 1984) found that children who had been together in the same classroom since they were about a year old got upset when some had to leave to start school. Even after their friends had gone the children left behind showed signs that they were unhappy. This project suggests that friendships made even at this early age may be important to children and that it is important to be sensitive to their feelings if these friendships are threatened.

Helping others

Part of the process of learning about getting on with other people is learning about their needs and feelings. As adults, our ideas about friendship usually involve some elements of sharing, helping, comforting and sympathizing. We also hold views about our responsibilities towards people less well off than ourselves and people who need our help. We make judgements about whether to contribute to famine appeals, whether to help someone who has fallen on the footpath, and whether to spend an evening with a friend who has a problem she would like to discuss. However, these behaviours are not exclusively characteristic of adults and more research evidence indicates that very young children try to respond to the needs of other people.

The term *prosocial behaviour* is used to describe any behaviour that is co-operative or that helps another or sympathizes with someone in distress. Although this behaviour is most obvious in older children and adults there is evidence that very young children respond when someone is upset. Although at first children cannot respond constructively when someone is upset they appear distressed. For example, an experiment has shown that newborn babies will cry if they hear the crying of another baby, suggesting that they are upset (see Radke-Yarrow, Zahn-Waxler and Chapman, 1983). This type of behaviour is seen throughout the first year of life. Six-month-old babies at first watched silently and then cried themselves when they were in the presence of another crying baby.

As children get older and are able to move around and can communicate with adults and friends, they display other types of prosocial behaviour. Twelve- and eighteen-month-old children will show toys or give them to other children or adults and will try to help with simple household tasks like sweeping the floor or folding clothes. They will also co-operate with older brothers and sisters in games or joint activities. In another experiment children approaching their second birthday made some attempts to help a distressed person by giving some form of reassurance or offering to get help.

How do children learn to behave prosocially?

No definite answer can be given as to why some children behave in a prosocial way when others do not, but it seems that a number of factors may have some influence (Radke-Yarrow, Zahn-Waxler and Chapman, 1983). The first factor is observation. Children learn by watching the actions of people around them and copying those actions themselves. In studies, children who observed an adult being generous were more likely to be generous themselves. Children tended to comfort one another in the way that they were comforted by their parents, suggesting that prosocial behaviour may be imitated. The second factor which seems to encourage prosocial behaviour is reward. Children who were praised when they helped another child were more likely to behave that way on another occasion. Finally, results from another experiment indicate that children will share with an adult if the adult makes a request to share with the child.

In any particular situation a child may be influenced by all of the above factors. When children were asked why they had helped another child they responded with a variety of reasons, including: (1) the other child needed something; (2) the other child was a friend; (3) to gain approval of another person; and (4) the helping behaviour would be of benefit to both children.

Problem behaviour

Behaviour which parents and day care workers find a concern or a problem is common in preschool and school-age children. When confronted with a child who has problem behaviour adults may have to decide whether the problem is serious enough to need special help or whether it is a problem that is likely to disappear as the child develops. Some problem behaviour cannot be overlooked because it affects many people, for example waking at night or aggression towards other children. Other forms of problem behaviour may not be so obvious but may, nevertheless, need help. Such a problem might be difficulty with taking part in group activity and therefore spending lots of time alone. Alternatively a child might be very unhappy but be unable to explain why.

When does a child need help?

When deciding whether or not a child needs help to overcome a particular problem a number of factors should be considered. The first is whether the child appears to have a problem which affects just one aspect of behaviour or which affects many. Research by Naomi Richman and her colleagues (Richman, Stevenson and Graham, 1982) suggests that an isolated problem, although distressing, is more likely to disappear over time than are a whole range of problems found in the same child. For example, children who wake at night are more likely to learn to sleep through the night if that is the only problem they have, than if it is accompanied by fearfulness, poor concentration and disobedience.

Also important when deciding what to do about problem behaviour is knowing what can reasonably be expected of children of different ages. Waking at night, crying when confronted by a stranger, and soiling are all features of a one-year-old's normal behaviour. Such behaviour would be of concern if it were observed in a four-year-old. We also know that certain types of problem behaviour such as temper tantrums are part of learning to be independent. Although such behaviour may be a problem to the child's caregiver it is part of a developmental process and should be handled as such.

Knowing about child development may be the first step in understanding a child's problem behaviour but knowing the individual child is also important. Difficult behaviour may occur around events such as the birth of a new brother or sister, a death in the family or going to a new childminder or nursery. Knowing what is happening to a child may help in understanding the problem.

What causes problem behaviour?

In the case of most problem behaviour no single cause will be found. Instead, there will be several factors that are likely to contribute to the child's behaviour (Richman, 1988). Sometimes it can be useful to think of the factors contributing to problem behaviour in terms of those arising from within the child and those arising from the child's immediate environment. Thinking of the situation in this way can help to identify which factors may be important.

Children differ in how tolerant they are of changes in their environment, how easily they settle into new routines and so on. These differences are sometimes referred to as differences in temperament. These differences will mean that two children going through exactly the same experience, for example changing to a new childminder, may react in very different ways. The child who easily settles to new routines and who tolerates change well will find the move much easier than a child who reacts strongly to new routines and who is only happy in very familiar environments. Understanding a child's temperament can help the adult to structure changes in such a way that they are made as easy as possible for the child.

Studies of problem behaviour indicate that a child's gender can have an effect on the likelihood of problem behaviour developing and persisting. Boys are more likely to develop problem behaviours than girls and they are also less likely to overcome the problems easily. Exactly why boys are more vulnerable in this way is not known but researchers suggest a number of possibilities. One possibility is that boys may not adapt so well to disruptions in their environments as girls. Another possibility is that boys may not receive as much support and comfort from adults as girls when confronted with difficult situations.

Poor child health is sometimes associated with problem behaviour. Children who are frequently ill are more likely to have problem behaviours than children who are healthy. These children may be coping with the stresses of pain or regular hospitalization and treatment and are therefore less able to cope with everyday stresses and frustrations.

Stress can also be caused by the home environment. Research has shown that children whose environments are stressful or unsupportive are more likely to develop problem behaviour than children whose environments are supportive. One aspect of the environment that can give rise to problem behaviour is frequent quarrelling between parents. Children seem to find this type of discord particularly difficult to cope with. Another factor in the environment which can give rise to problem behaviour is the presence of adults who themselves have problems with self-control and communication. Children learn a tremendous amount about social interaction from the adults with whom they live and if they live with adults who have these types of problem the child may learn these ways of behaving.

Part two: The effects of day care

Relationships and day care

Researchers who have studied the development of attachment relationships in young children have recently been asking the question 'Do children who enter full-time day care in the first year of life have problems in developing secure attachment relationships with their parents?' This is a good example of research led by psychological theory which was mentioned in Chapter 3. John Bowlby's theory of attachment has led some researchers to suggest that the daily separations from their parents experienced by children in day care in the first year might result in insecure attachment and later problem behaviour. Because more children in the USA, where most of this research has been undertaken, are attending day care from an early age this question has relevance for the development of many more children today than ten years ago. In some other countries the trend towards longer maternal and parental leave has meant that this question is of no relevance because so few children under a year old spend long periods of time in day care.

Researchers have tried to answer the question in two main ways. The first is to take two groups of children about one year old, one of which includes children who are attending full-time day care and one of which includes children who are not. Children in both groups are then studied in the *strange situation* with one or both parents. This allows researchers to say whether the children attending day care are more or less likely to be securely attached to their parents than the children not attending day care. The second way that researchers have tried to answer the question is by looking at the social and emotional development of older children who began attending day care before they were a year old and comparing them with children who never attended day care or who began attending day care when older. This allows the researchers to discover whether the children who attended day care were more prone to developing problem behaviour as predicted by attachment theory.

Attachment in infancy

Research which has studied the attachment security of children has mostly been carried out in the USA. Some of these studies have found that children in day care in the first year are less likely to be securely attached to their parents than children not attending day care. For example, one project collected information on 149 children (Belsky and Rovine, 1988). Both parents were interviewed about day care arrangements on three occasions:

when the children were three, nine and twelve months old. Just under half of the children were being looked after by their mothers at home, the rest of the children were in day care either full time (thirty-five hours or more per week), part time (twenty to thirty-five hours per week) or for a very short time each week (ten to twenty hours). The most commonly used day care was childminding, next most common was care in the child's home by a nanny; smaller numbers of children were cared for by relatives or were attending day nurseries.

Children took part in the *strange situation* with their mothers when they were twelve months old and with their fathers when they were thirteen months old. Children who were spending more time per week in day care were more likely to be classified as insecure in their attachment relationships. Also boys with more hours of day care were more likely to be insecurely attached to their fathers. Although insecure attachment was more common in these groups it should be noted that fewer than half of the children were insecurely attached. The project also found that there were differences in the personality and attitudes of the women which were associated with their attachment relationships with their children. In particular, mothers of insecurely attached infants were less sensitive, less positive about their marriages and expressed greater career motivation when their children were nine months old.

Findings like this have led some American researchers to campaign for longer periods of maternal and parental leave to permit full-time parental care in the first year of life. But others interpret these findings in a different way. They argue that children who have daily experience of separation from their parents cannot be expected to behave in the same way in the *strange situation* as children who spend every day at home. If children who spend every day in a nursery do not rush over to greet their mothers when they come back into the room during the procedure then that may be because they are not upset and do not want comfort. They argue that it is not appropriate to say that children behaving like that are insecurely attached. Maybe another way of measuring attachment for these children is needed.

Other researchers argue that the differences in attachment between children in day care and children at home are significant only in statistical terms, that is they can be detected mathematically but are small enough not to cause worry to the majority of parents and caregivers even if insecure attachment is assumed to have consequences for later development. After all, one-third of children who do not experience day care regularly are not securely attached.

Research on older children

The second way in which researchers have studied the effects of day care on developing attachment relationships has been to look at the development of older children. Three longitudinal research projects will be considered in this section, all of which followed the development of children at least until they started in primary school. The first project is the **FAST project** which was carried out in Sweden, the second is the **TCRU project** carried out in Britain and the third is the **Abecedarian project**.

The **FAST project** followed the development of a group of children from the age of three or four years right up to adolescence. The children were given regular developmental assessments and their mothers and teachers filled in questionnaires about their behaviour at home and at school. The researchers were particularly interested in the intellectual and social development of the children as they got older. Their results showed that when the children were eight years old, those who had attended day care were less anxious and more socially confident than other children. The research also suggested that children who began attending day care during their first year were less anxious and more socially confident than children who began attending day care when they were older.

The cognitive and language development of the children in the **TCRU project** has already been discussed in Chapters 4 and 5. Another interest of the researchers was the social development of the children. Throughout the project mothers completed questionnaires about their children's social and emotional behaviour. When the children were six years old, schoolteachers answered questions about positive and negative social behaviour in the classroom and the researchers who visited the children at home made notes on the children's behaviour.

The only differences between children who attended day care and children cared for at home were when the children were three years old. At this age the children who had attended day care were less timid and more sociable towards the researcher who visited them. The children who had attended day care were also more co-operative and seemed to have a more positive mood. When the children were six no differences were identified. The most likely reason for this is that by the time they were six almost all of the children had been to playgroup and to school. Thus all the children were used to meeting other children and adults. Questionnaires completed by mothers and teachers about problem behaviour at home and in school showed that there were again no differences between the children who had attended day care and the children who had been cared for at home.

There were some differences in the social development of the children in the different types of day care. When the children were eighteen months old those in the group attending day nurseries were less concerned on meeting an unfamiliar person than were the other children. They were also most upset if their mother left them temporarily, for example to go to another room. Again, when the children were three years old the nursery children had higher levels of sharing, co-operation and empathy with other children, but this difference was no longer found at age six.

Because some American research suggested that starting full-time day care during the first year might disrupt parent–infant attachment a small group of the children in the **TCRU project** took part in a special study of attachment when they were six years old. Half of the group had started attending day nursery during their first year, the other half spent their first year exclusively with their mothers. To make sure that the two groups were the same in other respects each child from the group which had attended a day nursery was matched with a child whose parents had a job of a similar level and who was the same sex and age and who had stayed at home. The children were visited at school and administered a short measure of attachment. No differences were found between the two groups of children. Researchers concluded that the experience of entering day care during their first year had not affected the attachment relationships or social development of these children.

The **Abecedarian project** is the final project to be considered and is the only one of the three to report increased aggression among children in day care. When the children had begun attending school, teachers' reports indicated that those who had attended the special day care were more aggressive than other children. This aggression included both verbal aggression (for example, arguing, teasing and threatening) and aggressive behaviour (including hitting, punching and kicking). However, not all of the children showed this increased level of aggression. Earlier in the project the workers had been concerned about levels of aggression, and a curriculum designed to reduce aggression was introduced for one small group of children. The main objectives of the curriculum were to eliminate problem behaviours and increase the frequency of positive social behaviours of the children. Activities were planned which would help to increase children's social understanding. At the same time staff received training in ways of managing problem behaviour. The curriculum was run for six months and then the behaviour of the children during playtime was observed. The observers found that aggressive behaviour had decreased by more than 90 per cent, suggesting that the curriculum and staff training had been very successful. These lower levels of aggression were confirmed by schoolteachers' reports when the children started primary school.

Does day care affect attachment?

In the last two sections research relevant to day care and attachment was discussed. The first section introduced research studies which have looked at the attachment relationships of children who are attending day care. One project was described which found that children who spent more time in day care during their first year were more likely to develop insecure attachment relationships. Although not all studies confirm this finding it is important to consider what such a finding might mean for the future development of the children involved. Will these children go on to develop problem behaviour as they get older? The second section considered this question using the results of studies which followed the development of children who began attending day care during their first year. The results of these studies were contradictory. One project found that the children who began attending day care before their first birthday were socially more advanced than the other children, the second project found no difference between the children in day care and the children at home, and the third project found that the children who began attending day care during their first year were more aggressive.

What explains these different findings? Each project was carried out in a different country so the levels of violence and the values of the societies in which the children and their families lived were different. This makes it difficult to decide whether the differences between the children were related to their day care experiences or to wider differences in the societies in which they lived. An additional complication is the fact that the children in the **Abecedarian project** all came from very poor backgrounds whereas the children in the other two studies came from families who had many more advantages; these differences may have contributed to the findings. It is also possible that the day care provided in the **Abecedarian project** may have been concentrating so much on encouraging the cognitive development of the children that little time was left to devote to social skills. After all, when the changes were made in the curriculum the levels of aggression dropped.

On balance, therefore, the results suggest that early entry into day care does not have long-term damaging consequences. The results of the **Abecedarian project** should, however, be taken as a reminder of the importance of social skills within the curriculum.

The role of caregivers

Moving away from the traditional concentration on attachment to parents, some recent research projects have investigated the relationship between children and their caregivers. The results of these projects were remarkably consistent. The results all agreed that children were more likely to be securely attached to their caregiver if the caregiver was sensitive to their needs. The **National Child Care Staffing Study** also found that children were more likely to be securely attached if they were responded to more often by their caregiver. Another American project (Howes *et al.*, 1988) found that a secure attachment relationship was encouraged in groups where there were fewer children. Perhaps a caregiver with fewer children to look after has more chance of being sensitive to the needs of individual children.

The **National Child Care Staffing Study** also looked at the effect of the caregivers' behaviour on other aspects of children's social development. It found that children were more likely to play at a more advanced level with others in their groups if their caregivers interacted with them. In common with the results presented in Chapters 4 and 5 the project also found that children's social development was encouraged by fewer changes in staff. In particular they found that in nurseries where staff did not stay for long the children were more likely to be found wandering aimlessly rather than playing with other children.

Social behaviour and day care

Children who spend time in day care typically come into contact with more non-family members than children at home with a parent. Children who attend day nurseries, in particular, spend a lot of time with other children. How do these experiences affect the children? Do they develop better social skills than children who do not have these opportunities? There is some evidence that children do learn social skills from their experiences in day care. In one American project (Field *et al.*, 1988) the children attended two high quality nurseries attached to universities. At the time of the study the average age of the children was about four years, though there were children younger and older than this. The results of this project suggested that children who had spent more time in day care were better at joining in group activities. Observers noted that the children who had been attending the day nurseries for longer spent less time playing alone and more time co-operating with other children. The children who had been there longer also appeared happier, they smiled and laughed more. These positive findings were confirmed in another project of high quality day care (Schindler, Moely and Frank, 1987). The researchers in this second project also found that children who had spent more time in day care joined with the other children more and were less likely to play alone or to remain as observers.

Increasing a child's tendency to join in group activities may also have negative consequences. Spending more time with other children may increase the chances of conflict. For example, the first project just reported (Field *et al.*, 1988) found that children who attended full-time day care were rated by teachers as more aggressive and assertive than those who attended part time. The second project (Schindler, Moely and Frank, 1987) found no such difference. In the discussion of day care and attachment above it was mentioned that the teachers of children in the **Abecedarian project** thought that the children who had attended the special day care were more aggressive. Why should some studies report aggressive behaviour and not others? One possibility is that by increasing social interaction with other children day care also increases the likelihood of aggression. Although this is possible it is unlikely to account for the results because if it were true then most studies of day care would report increased aggression and they do not.

Perhaps some day care environments are more likely to result in the children behaving aggressively towards one another. It was already mentioned in discussion of the **Abecedarian project** that a change in curriculum influenced the level of aggressive behaviour. Further evidence that the environment influences aggression comes from a British project (Smith and Connolly, 1977) which looked specifically at situations which encourage aggression. In this project two groups of children in a playgroup were studied over a year to see what factors in the classroom environment would affect their social behaviour. They found that there were some changes in the ways that children played if the amount of available space was decreased; for example, they were less likely to engage in rough-and-tumble play. Their most striking finding was that decreasing the amount of play equipment increased the number of aggressive behaviours observed. Most of the observed increase in aggression was due to conflicts over limited equipment. Taken together these studies suggest that careful attention should be given to the environment provided for children and to the ways in which the children are encouraged to behave if levels of aggression are to be kept to a minimum.

Emotional development and day care

In addition to collecting information on the social development of children many studies also collect information on the children's emotional development including their self-concept, happiness, independence and so on. In one project carried out in the USA questionnaires were sent to the parents and teachers of over 200 eight-year-olds (Vandell and Corasaniti, 1990). Questions covered such areas as friendships, happiness, fearfulness, co-operativeness and obedience. Teachers were asked to answer questions about each child's progress in school and parents also answered questions about day care experience including the type of day care attended by the children (if any), how many hours per week they had attended, how old they were when they had started. The results of the project were quite negative for children who had attended day care. These children were reported by both parents and teachers to be less compliant, that is they were less likely to do things asked of them. Teachers also reported that the children who had attended day care were more fearful, less open, less interested and less happy. The researchers suggest that one explanation for these findings may be the poor quality of day care in Texas where they did the research. Childminders there may look after as many as twelve children (including four babies) single-handed. In day nurseries the situation is very little better with ratios of one adult to six children under a year old and one adult to eighteen four-year-olds. Although many day nurseries and childminders may have better ratios, those are the minimum legal requirements. Such low legal standards are obviously not conducive to a high general standard of care. In addition, because the data were collected retrospectively it is not possible to say whether the differences were due to differences in the families when choosing day care.

Negative results like those just described are not typical of the research findings on the emotional development of children who have attended day care. Two large-scale longitudinal studies which do not confirm these findings have already been discussed. The results of the **FAST project** were very positive about the development of children who attended day care, particularly those children who began attending day care before they were a year old. These children were more persistent and independent than other children when they were eight years old. The results of the **TCRU project** also found no negative effects on the social development of children who had attended day care in Britain. When the children were six, information from their mothers was collected on aspects of their emotional development and the researchers used a measure of the children's feelings of competence. The children who attended day care were no different from the children who did not.

Day care and problem behaviour

Almost all parents and people who work with children are going to encounter a child with problems at some stage. Because parents and caregivers see children in different environments and make different demands on children they will often find that they are not in agreement on which children have problems and which do not. For example, parents may find that problems with waking during the night are the most disruptive to their family life and may be a matter of great concern. Day care workers may be more concerned about the inability of a child to socialize with other children in the group. Because parents do not often see their child in a group of children they may be unaware that their child has a problem.

Most studies which are interested in levels of problem behaviour ask parents and/or teachers to fill out questionnaires about common problems. Based on the answers children attending day care (or children who used to attend day care) can be compared with children who do not (or who did not) attend day care to see if there are differences in rates of problem behaviour in the two groups. This method was used in the **TCRU project** when the children were three years old and again when they were six. The results of the project found no difference in levels of problem behaviour at either age between the children who had attended day care and the children who had been cared for at home. In other words a child who had attended day care was no more likely to have behaviour problems than a child cared for at home.

The **TCRU project** is not the only project to have found no relationship between day care attendance and problem behaviour. In Carollee **Howes's** study of day care quality, teachers were asked to complete questionnaires about the problem behaviour of the four-year-old children in their class. Most of the children had attended some form of day care before beginning school and the researchers were able to rate the day care arrangements for quality. Day care arrangements were rated as high quality if there were small groups of children (fewer than twenty-five), high adult:child ratio (one adult to no more than eight children), if each child had an individual educational programme and enough physical space. The results of the project indicated that children who had attended higher quality day care programmes had lower levels of problem behaviour.

Summary of day care research

(1) There is some evidence that children who attend full-time day care during their first year are more likely to be classified as having insecure attachments to their parents. The interpretation of this finding is controversial because most long-term studies of children in day care find no evidence that it has harmed their social development.
(2) Children are more likely to be securely attached to their caregiver if the caregiver is sensitive to their needs.
(3) Environmental features and activities in day care affect the levels of aggressive behaviour observed in groups of children.
(4) Children who attend group-based day care (such as day nurseries) are more likely to join in group activities.
(5) Children who attend high quality day care have similar levels of problem behaviour to children who do not attend. There is also some evidence that attending low quality day care may be associated with higher levels of problem behaviour.

Suggested further reading

Rutter, M. (1986) *Maternal Deprivation Reassessed*, Penguin, Harmondsworth.

Schaffer, H. R. (1984) *The Child's Entry into a Social World*, Academic Press, London.

Richman, N. and Lansdown, R. (eds.) (1988) *Problems of Preschool Children*, Wiley, Chichester.

7

RESEARCH AND PRACTICE: PAST LESSONS, FUTURE PARTNERSHIPS

The last three chapters have reviewed research which has looked at the impact of day care attendance on children's development. This concluding chapter summarizes the results from this research, identifying areas of agreement and disagreement, and considers some of the implications for practice in day care services. Finally, the chapter looks to the future, proposing a number of areas which need more attention from researchers and suggesting one approach which might help to resolve the long-standing problem of how to develop a productive relationship and partnership between researchers and practitioners.

What effects does day care attendance have on children?

At a general level the answer to this question seems to be 'very little'. The conclusion to be drawn from many research studies going back over many years is that the simple fact of attending day care has no inherent effect on children, either for better or worse. Those seeking important influences on children's development should look elsewhere, for example to factors such as social class. Children do not require full-time parental care, even at an early age, and are capable of forming satisfactory and satisfying attachments with a number of caregivers, both parents and others. Moreover, there is no reason to think that any one type of day care is inherently better or worse for children's development and well-being than any other; no project has found differences in children attending different types of day care which could not be explained by some other factor.

Fortunately, at least for researchers' livelihoods, this is not the end of the story. For within this broad conclusion there are a number of important exceptions and qualifications. While there is no inevitable consequence of day care, in certain conditions it can have an effect on children. Four main conditions emerge from the research done so far.

Home circumstances

Day care, like preschool education, can be beneficial for children from disadvantaged homes, promoting optimum development. This suggests that where there is a large discrepancy between the quality of care provided in the home and in day care, day care attendance will have an effect. For example, good day care can compensate for deficiencies in home experience, whilst extremely poor day care might undermine the effects of a good home environment. Where day care and home are roughly equivalent then day care experience will have little effect.

Caregiver behaviour

The behaviour of caregivers can affect the development of children. For example, children are more likely to be securely attached to caregivers who are warm and sensitive; children's cognitive and language development are more likely to be advanced where caregivers engage in one-to-one conversations; children cared for by more responsive caregivers have more advanced language development; children benefit from caregivers providing developmentally appropriate learning opportunities and other experiences. In short, adults who are responsive and sensitive to children and their stage of development promote children's further development. This is true whether the adults are parents or workers in day care services.

Stability of care

This is beginning to emerge as an important factor in the development of children, with evidence accumulating that instability can have negative effects whether caused by frequent changes in day care setting or frequent changes of workers within the setting. However, the exact implications need further study. In particular, we need to know more about how far the problem lies in the instability of care itself (for example, lack of consistency in care received, the upset to children that sudden and unanticipated change can bring) or in the factors which create instability. For example, poor working conditions might promote a lack of responsiveness and sensitivity among workers in a particular day care setting. The same conditions might also lead to instability of care due to high staff turnover among those workers. The development of children in that setting might be affected by the lack of responsiveness or the high staff turnover – or a combination of both factors.

Children's age

There remains some controversy about whether admission to full-time day care before twelve months of age may increase the possibility of an insecure child–parent attachment, which in turn may be associated with certain problems of social development in later childhood. The controversy therefore is not about any type of day care, but about full-time attendance for very young children. The evidence supporting the view that day care may carry this risk is from the USA and has used a measure of attachment whose appropriateness has been questioned.

What lessons can be drawn?

A good day care setting

Day care settings which promote children's development and well-being share a number of features. Adults working in the settings will show warmth, affection and consistency to the children. There will be lots of communication, with the adults being responsive to the children. There will be learning opportunities, to improve the basic knowledge of children about the world and to give them new skills. This means providing developmentally appropriate experiences, which change as children develop and which are varied enough to prevent boredom. Most important, children's talent for self-initiated learning and curiosity about the world should be nurtured.

Effective day care settings will be stable, in the sense that children are not moved elsewhere unless appropriate (for example, because they have reached the age to move on to school) and are with a small and constant group of caregivers. In such stable settings, children are more likely to experience consistent and responsive relationships. They should also be able to form attachments to several caregivers, each of whom can be used as a secure base for the children to explore their environments, and each of whom will understand the context and individual nature of the children's communications and behaviour and so be able to respond appropriately. Where change of placement or caregiver cannot be avoided, careful attention should be paid to managing the transition.

Finally, but equally important, are relationships between children. From an early age, children enjoy and respond to the company of other children.

Day care settings should provide opportunities for interaction with other children, because children enjoy this and because there is some evidence that it improves social skills. A particularly valuable sort of interaction is with familiar children, in other words within a circle of friends. Because of the way that day care is normally organized, these friends will usually be around the same age; however, children may also enjoy and gain from the company of children substantially younger or older than themselves (for example, children under three having the opportunity to meet children of primary or secondary school age).

The right conditions for developing good day care settings

The features of a good day care setting outlined above are more likely to develop if certain conditions are present. For example, warm, responsive and stable adult–child relationships and appropriate learning opportunities are more likely if a range of features are found. These include: a well-organized and stimulating physical environment; a range of suitable activities; a trained and stable workforce, with proper pay and conditions of employment; an appropriate group size and adult:child ratios; and where children's access to such environments, and continuity of care within them, does not depend on parents' jobs, the ability of parents to pay, or other factors unrelated to the needs of the children. These conditions, in turn, require adequate funding so that accommodation, equipment and materials, the training, pay and conditions of the workforce, and the provision of support services to assist with training and curriculum development can all be properly resourced. To take just one link in the chain, children's experience and well-being in day care is affected by staff behaviour which in turn is affected by pay, conditions and training, which in turn again depends on the level of resourcing for services and training.

The level of resources allocated to day care services and how equally and effectively these resources are allocated between individual settings is, in part, a consequence of government policies. These policies in turn form an important part of the wider context that was discussed in Chapter 1. Sense cannot be made of research findings without taking account of the broad economic, social and political context within which individual day care services operate, and which determines not only how much day care is used but also what type and quality of day care is available to which children. Context varies from place to place even within the 'developed' world – the USA is very different from Denmark, France very different from Britain. Context also varies over time, as economic, social and political circumstances change. What we do and believe today will seem as distant to researchers in 100 years time as Victorian beliefs and behaviour do to us now. An essential lesson for researchers and practitioners alike is the danger of generalizing research findings without taking account of differences in context.

Where are the gaps in research?

Quality

Currently there is a lot of interest in the quality of day care services. This mainly involves work focusing on how best to promote certain aspects of children's development (cognitive, language, social and emotional). When researchers say that there is a relationship between day care quality and the effects of day care on children they mean that research findings have shown that certain features of day care settings (such as the way workers communicate with the children) promote development; or that certain conditions (such as staff:child ratios or staff training and pay) are associated with better developmental results, probably because they encourage responsive communication or other positive features of day care settings.

This is clearly an important area and justifies further work. There would probably be widespread agreement that day care settings should promote development, but, important as this is, this objective is only one of a number of objectives which might be set for day care and which could be included in work on 'day care quality'. Indeed, in some ways the word 'quality' is not particularly helpful when thinking about future research. As with 'justice', 'beauty' and 'virtue', we all believe in 'quality' and support it as a 'good thing'. However, as with 'justice', 'beauty' and 'virtue', there is considerable scope for disagreement when it comes to deciding what we mean by the term 'quality', for the very good reason that any definition is based necessarily on personal beliefs and values. The value basis of any definition of quality is recognized in the Guidance and Regulations produced by the Department of Health (1991b, p. 40) for the day care sections of the 1989 Children Act: 'deciding whether services . . . are of acceptable quality involves a value judgement. There should be a clear understanding about the value base and the criteria used for assessing quality of care in these situations.'

Perhaps it is more useful to proceed by dropping the term 'quality' or agreeing to use it specifically in relation to promoting children's cognitive, language, social and emotional development. In its place, or supplementing this specific definition, we can refer to objectives; a good day care setting would be one that achieved its agreed objectives. The task then becomes to define objectives for day care (which may cover a potentially wide range of aims concerning children, parents, the local community, and so on), and to use research skills to understand how best to achieve defined objectives as well as to develop methods for monitoring the achievement of objectives.

Day care workers

Day care workers have a vital role – probably *the* vital role – to play in achieving the objectives of the services in which they work. Regular information is needed on the training, pay and conditions, job satisfaction and turnover across all types of care including grandmothers, nannies, childminders and day nurseries. More specifically, research should focus on the conditions necessary to enable workers in day care settings to work effectively.

Care arrangements and histories

Information needs to be collected regularly on how children are being cared for (taking into account all the components in their care both at home and elsewhere, by parents and others), and how and why these arrangements change over time (what we described in Chapter 1 as day care histories). Against this background, research is needed which looks more carefully at the relationship between the different people and settings involved in caring for individual children. Additionally we need to understand the conditions under which change may be detrimental (or even in some cases, positive) and how best to manage change.

Difference and 'otherness'

Many countries are ethnically diverse. In addition to ethnicity, there are many other important dimensions of diversity in all populations using day care services, such as gender, social class, language, the type of area in which families live (for example rural, suburban, inner city) and children with special needs. More research is needed on the relationship between these dimensions and day care. Some research may focus specifically on one of these dimensions, for example looking at how gender affects children's experience of day care or the day care needs of families in rural areas.

But a broader approach is also needed. Future research needs to be based on a recognition that diversity and 'otherness' are central features of contemporary society. Whether we are looking at what parents want in the way of day care, what happens to children in day care, or at workers in day care, research needs to recognize and reflect the diversity of society and consider how far day care experience is different for children and parents from different groups.

The costs and structure of services

Chapter 1 referred to how the division between day care and education services for preschool children, under and over three years old, was being questioned. It was mentioned that some initiatives had been taken to integrate all early childhood services within one administrative structure, replacing previous divisions between education and welfare, and that these developments challenge traditional ways of thinking about services. Such developments are still not widespread, but indicate important trends. If they are to be taken further, many practical issues need to be tackled concerning the organization and structuring of services and training, within an integrated system of 'early childhood services'. There is the further challenge of developing flexible and multifunctional services, which combine care and education and meet a wide range of needs of children and their parents.

Any discussion or review of the quantity, quality and organization of services raises important cost issues. What is the cost of providing good early childhood services? What are the off-setting benefits for children, mothers, fathers, employers and society as a whole? How should costs be shared between parents, employers and society (government)? How should public funding be allocated – by tax relief on parents' costs, the subsidy of parents' fees or direct funding of services themselves? To what extent is there a role for both private and publicly funded day care? How can public and privately funded day care be integrated to provide a coherent range of services for young children? Researchers have an important part to play, in collaboration with others, in the development of new services and structures and in seeking answers to these cost questions.

Cross-national studies

This book has included research undertaken in three countries (mainly the USA, but also Britain and Sweden). National comparisons are important because they reveal the importance of context in determining children's day care experiences and in interpreting research results. There remain, however, two major gaps. First, there are many countries about which no research findings have been reported in this book. In some cases this may be because research results have been published in languages other than English and not, therefore, in one of the English-language academic journals which dominate the field of psychology and child development. But it is also because there has been little research on the effects of day care undertaken in a number of interesting countries (for example Denmark).

Second, in addition to knowing more about specific countries, more cross-national research is needed, that is studies which include and contrast day care settings in more than one country, for example comparing nurseries in, say, Denmark and Italy or Germany and Ireland. Such work would contribute to our understanding both of the impact of context and of the different ideas and objectives in working with young children.

Childhood

Research has indicated that the impact of day care may depend to some extent on the child's home. Researchers increasingly recognize that day care settings cannot be studied in isolation from the home, the local community, the wider society and so on. They must be looked at in terms of how they fit into the wider picture of how children are cared for and brought up, and how they relate to the wider world outside day care services.

This recognition is already influencing research and should continue to do so. For example, the supply of day care workers and their current conditions and training can only be understood in the wider context of women's employment and the demand for women in the labour force. Children's total experience – their everyday lives – and how day care relates to other parts of children's lives need to be better understood. The starting point for defining day care quality or objectives should be to consider 'quality of everyday life' for children, and what objectives we set ourselves for childhood. This broader perspective provides a framework within which objectives for day care can be better and more easily defined.

This has policy implications. If day care services are seen as part of a child's overall care arrangements, other policies which affect these arrangements need to be considered alongside day care services. For example, the development of parental leave (described in Chapter 1) has implications for the use of day care for very young children, as does the organization of working life and the division of children's care between mothers and fathers. A policy package to reconcile the care of young children with parental employment and equality of opportunity for women would need to promote not only good day care services but also a range of leave arrangements (paternity leave, leave to care for sick children, as well as parental and maternity leave), the creation of more 'parent-friendly' workplaces and increased participation by men in children's care.

This broad, holistic approach to children and their care will inevitably affect thinking not only about day care policy, but also about day care itself. Instead of regarding day care as a substitute for home care, with research focusing on whether this substitution harms children, day care can be seen as one of a number of care settings that contribute to children's total experience. Taking this approach, research can ask more subtle questions, focusing on how different care settings relate to each other, how day care fits into the child's wider experience, and the specific contribution of day care to that experience. This broad perspective has been adopted in a recent project of the everyday life of young children in the Nordic countries which illustrates how home circumstances can affect children's experience in day care. The Danish researchers in this cross-national project conclude:

> A very large proportion of the young children in the Nordic countries live in more than one world which will influence their development. One consequence is that it becomes difficult to explain the child's new reality with such concepts as primary socialisation and secondary socialisation.
>
> Instead we prefer to call the situation in which the child finds itself, a 'dual socialisation situation'. The child transfers the experience gained in one environment to the other and vice versa . . . One of the environments assumes meaning for the child in a way which is dependent on how this element of experience is integrated into the total configuration of experience . . .
>
> What is crucial is not what is experienced in the daycare centre itself, but how this fits into the whole life-pattern of experience which the child has. The decisive factors are the time-allocation of work that the parents have and the nature of the family structure.
>
> (Elgaard *et al.*, 1989, pp. 13–14)

Is partnership between research and practice possible?

Much of the research on the agenda outlined above will be undertaken by academic researchers, who will continue to be concerned with research involving both theory and more general applied issues. It is important that the results of their work are widely read and understood, through a variety of channels including training for day care workers. But, however successful this dissemination, such research will not necessarily have an impact on day care practice. For the problem is not primarily one of dissemination or presentation. Jerome Bruner, an eminent researcher who tried hard to influence practice and policy through dissemination, came to recognize this.

> Why was dissemination so baffling? Why did all of this compiled [research] knowledge have so little effect on childcare practice and policy? That was the question that gave me pause . . . 'Dissemination' is the wrong metaphor for making research useful in the climate of childcare. It smacks of spreading the word to the uninitiated . . . There is presently no available way of gearing child research into this effort of self-improvement in child-rearing.
>
> (Bruner, 1980, pp. xiv and 215)

As Bruner concluded, the issue is more fundamental than how best to disseminate findings. Ways must be found to make research an integral part of services. To do this and develop an effective partnership with practice, new types of research relationship need to be developed.

The questions that academic researchers attempt to answer will emerge usually from within the world of scientific research or perhaps from government departments. They will be questions that are of a general nature rather than particular to a specific day care setting or service. Such work is necessary and important. But it needs to be supplemented by research which is at the service of practitioners and others engaged on a day-to-day basis with the running, development and improvement of day care settings. In this capacity researchers can contribute in a number of ways. For example, they can assist with the analysis of problems and offer advice on how to resolve them, provide information through surveys of families or workers and evaluate alternative methods or approaches. They can be an important source for helping practitioners and others assess need, make decisions, monitor performance and tackle problems.

In order for researchers to make this contribution and become an integral part of the life of services, those who work in services need to be able to identify where research can be helpful and to discuss with researchers what contribution they can make. This means that day care workers must have some understanding of research and its role and also a critical appreciation of the limitations of research.

Two other conditions need to be met if research is to make a substantial and integral contribution to services. First, resources must be allocated for this purpose. At present, expenditure on research on day care constitutes a minute proportion of the total expenditure on these services (less than 0.01 per cent). Second, if more money is to be spent on research, to help practically in the improvement of services, then new ways must be found of allocating these resources.

There are two ways of achieving this. First, services should have funds earmarked for spending on research needs that they identify. These funds could be used to buy in expertise or employ researchers on a regular basis.

Research might vary from a small-scale, short-term study of a particular problem in a particular day care setting or group of settings to a consortium of agencies funding a relatively large-scale project. Whatever the scale or level of work, the important point is that initiatives come from within services themselves; they might come from managers or from a group of day care workers who feel the need for assistance in the setting where they work.

Second, service-providing agencies should incorporate research into the process of developing and implementing new services or new approaches. This research and development model is familiar in industry, indeed it is essential to the success of many companies. This role in day care could be undertaken by outsiders, bidding for a specific contract to do the research, or by an internal research and development group, employed directly by the agency. The important issue is that those working in the services are involved in determining the direction of the research. The researchers and others contribute to the process of service development, evaluation and implementation.

As researchers, we want to see research play a more important role in ensuring that day care meets its objectives and contributes to improving the quality of life of children, their parents and workers in services. To be more influential, research will have to seek more equal relationships with people who work in and with the services with which research is concerned. Day care workers and others need to know what lessons research has for them, but must also understand the limitations and problems of research. They need, in short, to be helped to develop a critical appreciation of the role of research in general and the results of specific studies in particular. Above all, practitioners and others need to be active initiators of research and partners who can see and use research for what it is – a useful tool to assist in the complex and important business of working with young children.

REFERENCES

Andersson, B-E. (1989) Effects of public day-care; a longitudinal study, *Child Development*, Vol. 60, pp. 857–66.

Andersson, B-E. (1990) Intellectual and socio-emotional competence in Swedish schoolchildren related to early child care. Poster presented at the 4th European Conference on Developmental Psychology, University of Stirling, 27–31 August.

Arend, R., Gove, F. L. and Sroufe, L. A. (1979) Continuity of individual adaptation from infancy to kindergarten: a predictive study of ego-resiliency and curiosity in preschoolers, *Child Development*, Vol. 50, pp. 950–9.

Belsky, J. and Rovine, M. J. (1988) Nonmaternal care in the first year of life and the security of infant–parent attachment, *Child Development*, Vol. 59, pp. 157–67.

Bower, T. G. R., Broughton, J. M. and Moore, M. K. (1971) Development of the object concept as manifested in the tracking behaviour of infants between 7 and 20 weeks of age, *Journal of Experimental Child Psychology*, Vol. 11, pp. 182–93.

Bowlby, J. (1971) *Attachment and Loss*, Vol. 1, *Attachment*, Pelican, Aylesbury.

Bowlby, J. (1975) *Attachment and Loss*, Vol. 2, *Separation, Anxiety and Anger*, Pelican, Aylesbury.

Brannen, J. and Moss, P. (1990) *Managing Mothers: Dual Earner Households after Maternity Leave*, Unwin Hyman, London.

Broberg, A., Hwang, C-P., Lamb, M. E. and Ketterlinus, R. D. (1989) Child care effects on socioemotional and intellectual competence in Swedish preschoolers, in J. S. Lande, S. Scarr and N. Gunzenhauser (eds.) *Caring for Children*, Erlbaum, Hillsdale, New Jersey.

Broberg, A. and Hwang, P. (1990) Day care for young children in Sweden, in E. Melhuish and P. Moss (eds.) *Day Care for Young Children: International Perspectives*, Routledge, London.

Bruner, J. (1980) *Under Five in Britain*, Grant McIntyre, London.

Burchinal, M., Lee, M. and Ramey, C. (1989) Type of day-care and preschool intellectual development in disadvantaged children, *Child Development*, Vol. 60, pp. 128–37.

Burns, V. (1989) Early childhood education in New Zealand – the quiet revolution. Paper given at the OMEP XIX World Assembly, London University, July.

Central Statistical Office (1991) *Social Trends 1991*, CSO, London.

Clarke-Stewart, K. A. (1987a) In search of consistencies in child care research, in D. A. Phillips (ed.) *Quality in Child Care: What Does Research Tell Us?* NAEYC, New York.

Clarke-Stewart, K. A. (1987b) Predicting child development from child care forms and features: the Chicago study, in D. A. Phillips (ed.) *Quality in Child Care: What Does Research Tell Us?* NAEYC, New York.

Clarke-Stewart, A. (1991) Day care in the USA, in P. Moss and E. Melhuish (eds.) *Current Issues in Day Care for Young Children*, HMSO, London.

Dawson, D. (1990) *Child Care Arrangements, Advance Data from Vital and Health Statistics* of the National Center for Health Statistics, Department of Health and Human Resources, Hyattsville, Maryland.

De Casper, A. J. and Fifer, W. P. (1980) Of human bonding; newborns prefer their mothers' voices, *Science*, Vol. 208, pp. 1174–6.

Dencik, L. (1989) Growing up in the post – modern age, *Acta Sociologica*, Vol. 32, pp. 155–80.

Department of Health (1991a) *Children's Day Care Facilities at 31 March 1990*, Department of Health, London.

Department of Health (1991b) *The Children Act 1989 Guidance and Regulations*, Vol. 2, HMSO, London.

Desai, S., Chase-Lansdale, P. L. and Michael, R. T. (1989) Mother or market? Effects of maternal employment on the intellectual ability of four-year-old children, *Demography*, Vol. 24, pp. 545–61.

Donaldson, M. (1978) *Children's Minds*, Fontana, London.

Education Select Committee (House of Commons) (1989a) *Educational Provision for the Under Fives*, Vol. I, HMSO, London.

Education Select Committee (House of Commons) (1989b) *Educational Provision for the Under Fives*, Vol. II, HMSO, London.

Elgaard, E., Langsted, O. and Sommer, D. (eds.) (1989) *Research on Socialisation of Young Children in the Nordic Countries*, Aarhus University Press, Aarhus.

Field, T. (1984) Separation stress of young children transferring to new school, *Developmental Psychology*, Vol. 20, pp. 786–92.

Field, T., Masi, W., Goldstein, S., Perry, S. and Parl, S. (1988) Infant day care facilitates preschool social behavior, *Early Childhood Research Quarterly*, Vol. 3, pp. 341–59.

Gathorne-Hardy, J. (1972) *The Rise and Fall of the British Nanny*, Hodder & Stoughton, London.

Goelman, H. and Pence, A. R. (1987) Effects of child care, family and individual characteristics on children's language development: the Victoria day care research project, in D. A. Phillips (ed.) *Quality in Child Care: What Does Research Tell Us?* NAEYC, New York.

Goelman, H. and Pence, A. R. (1988) Children in three types of day care: daily experiences, quality of care and developmental outcomes, *Early Child Development and Care*, Vol. 33, pp. 67–76.

Haskins, R. (1985) Public school aggression among children with varying day-care experience, *Child Development*, Vol. 56, pp. 689–703.

Hennessy, E., Martin, S., Moss, P. and Melhuish, E. (1990) Social development at six years as a function of type and amount of early child care. Paper given at the Child Care in the Early Years Conference, University of Lausanne, 12–14 September.

Hobsbawm, E. (1987) *The Age of Capital*, Weidenfeld, London.

Howes, C. (1988) Relations between early child care and schooling, *Developmental Psychology*, Vol. 24, pp. 53-7.

Howes, C., Rodning, C., Galluzzo, D. C. and Myers, L. (1988) Attachment and child care: relationships with mother and caregiver, *Early Childhood Research Quarterly*, Vol. 3, pp. 403–16.

Langsted, O. and Sommer, D. (in press) Changing socialisation patterns, child care policies and programmes in contemporary Denmark in M.Cochran (ed.) *International Handbook of Day Care Policies and Programmes*, Greenwood, New York.

Leprince, F. (1990) Day care for young children in France, in E. Melhuish and P. Moss (eds.) *Day Care for Young Children: International Perspectives*, Routledge, London.

McCartney, K. (1984) Effect of quality of day care environment on children's language development, *Developmental Psychology*, Vol. 20, pp. 244–60.

Martin, S., Hennessy, E., Melhuish, E. and Moss, P. (1990) Attachment at six – does early daycare really matter? Poster presented at the 4th European Conference on Developmental Psychology, University of Stirling, 27–31 August.

Mayall, B. and Petrie, P. (1977) *Minder, Mother and Child*, University of London Institute of Education, London.

Melhuish, E. C. (1991) Research on day care for young children in the United Kingdom, in E. C. Melhuish and P. Moss (eds.) *Day Care for Young Children: International Perspectives*, Routledge, London.

Melhuish, E. C., Lloyd, E., Martin, S. and Mooney, A. (1990) Type of childcare at 18 months. II. Relations with cognitive and language development, *Journal of Child Psychology and Psychiatry*, Vol. 31, pp. 861–70.

Melhuish, E. and Moss, P. (eds.) (1991) *Day Care for Young Children: International Perspectives*, Routledge, London.

Milne, A. M., Myers, D. E., Rosenthal, A. S. and Ginsburg, A. (1986) Single parents, working mothers, and the educational achievement of school children, *Sociology of Education*, Vol. 59, pp. 125–39.

Moss, P. (1987) *A Review of Childminding Research*. TCRU Occasional and Research Paper No. 7, Thomas Coram Research Unit, London.

Moss, P. (1988) *Childcare and Equality of Opportunity*, European Commission, Brussels.

Moss, P. (1990) *Childcare in the European Communities, 1985–1990*, European Commission, Brussels.

Parten, M. B. (1932) Social participation among preschool children, *Journal of Abnormal and Social Psychology*, Vol. 27, pp. 243–69.

Phillips, D. (1987) Epilogue, in D. Phillips (ed.) *Quality in Child Care: What Does Research Tell Us*? NAEYC, New York.

Phillips, D. (1990) Day care for young children in the United States, in E. C. Melhuish and P. Moss (eds.) *Day Care for Young Children: International Perspectives*, Routledge, London.

Radke-Yarrow, M., Zahn-Waxler, C. and Chapman, M. (1983) Prosocial dispositions and behavior, in P. Mussen (ed.) *Manual of Child Psychology*, Vol. 4, *Socialization, Personality and Social Development*, Wiley, New York.

Richman, N. (1988) Overview of behaviour and emotional problems, in N. Richman and R. Lansdown (eds.) *Problems of Preschool Children*, Wiley, Chichester.

Richman, N., Stevenson, J. and Graham, P. J. (1982) *Pre-School to School: A Behavioural Study*, Academic Press, London.

Rubenstein, J. L. and Howes, C. (1979) Caregiving and infant behavior in day care and in homes, *Developmental Psychology*, Vol. 15, pp. 1–24.

Schaffer, H. R. and Emerson, P. E. (1964) The development of social attachments in infancy, *Monographs of the Society for Research in Child Development*, Vol. 29, no. 3.

Schindler, P. J., Moely, B. E. and Frank, A. L. (1987) Time in day care and social participation of young children, *Developmental Psychology*, Vol. 23, pp. 255–61.

Smith, P. K. and Connolly, K. J. (1977) Social and aggressive behaviour in preschool children as a function of crowding, *Social Science Information*, Vol. 16, pp. 601–20.

Snow, C. (1977) The development of conversation between mothers and babies, *Journal of Child Language*, Vol. 4, pp. 1–22.

Sroufe, L. A., Fox, N. E. and Pancake, V. R. (1983) Attachment and dependency in developmental perspective, *Child Development*, Vol. 54, pp. 1615–27.

Trehub, S.E. and Rabinovitch, M.S. (1972) Auditory-linguistic sensitivity in early infancy, *Developmental Psychology*, Vol. 6, pp. 74–7.

Vandell, D. L. and Corasaniti, M. A. (1990) Variations in early child care: do they predict subsequent social, emotional, and cognitive differences? *Early Childhood Research Quarterly*, Vol. 5, pp. 555–72.

Wasik, B. H., Ramey, C. T., Bryant, D. M. and Sparling, J. J. (1990) A longitudinal study of two early intervention strategies: Project CARE, *Child Development*, Vol. 61, pp. 1682–96.

Whitebook, M., Howes, C. and Phillips, D. (1989) *Who Cares? Child Care Teachers and the Quality of Care in America*. Final report of the National Child Care Staffing Study, Child Care Employee Project, Oakland, California.

INDEX